Composition for Computer Musicians

Michael Hewitt

Course Technology PTR
A part of Cengage Learning

COURSE TECHNOLOGY
CENGAGE Learning

Australia • Brazil • Japan • Korea • Mexico • Singapore • Spain • United Kingdom • United States

COURSE TECHNOLOGY
CENGAGE Learning™

Composition for Computer Musicians
Michael Hewitt

Publisher and General Manager, Course Technology PTR: Stacy L. Hiquet

Associate Director of Marketing: Sarah Panella

Manager of Editorial Services: Heather Talbot

Marketing Manager: Mark Hughes

Executive Editor: Mark Garvey

Development Editor: Cathleen D. Small

Project Editor/Copy Editor: Cathleen D. Small

Editorial Services Coordinator: Jen Blaney

Interior Layout Tech: Macmillan Publishing Solutions

Cover Designer: Luke Fletcher

CD-ROM Producer: Brandon Penticuff

Indexer: Broccoli Information Management

Proofreader: Heather Urschel

For product information and technology assistance, contact us at
Cengage Learning Customer & Sales Support, 1-800-354-9706

For permission to use material from this text or product, submit all requests online at **www.cengage.com/permissions**
Further permissions questions can be emailed to
permissionrequest@cengage.com

All trademarks are the property of their respective owners.

Library of Congress Control Number: 2008935089

ISBN-13: 978-1-59863-861-5

ISBN-10: 1-59863-861-0

Course Technology, a part of Cengage Learning
20 Channel Center Street
Boston, MA 02210
USA

Cengage Learning is a leading provider of customized learning solutions with office locations around the globe, including Singapore, the United Kingdom, Australia, Mexico, Brazil, and Japan. Locate your local office at:
international.cengage.com/region

Cengage Learning products are represented in Canada by Nelson Education, Ltd.

For your lifelong learning solutions, visit **courseptr.com**

Visit our corporate website at **cengage.com**

Printed in the United States of America
7 8 16 15 14

This book is dedicated to Coleg Harlech WEA, North Wales (http://www.harlech.ac.uk/en/)—may it long continue to provide vital adult education.

Acknowledgments

Thanks are due to Mark Garvey, for his sympathetic handling of this project; Cathleen Small, for her brilliant development editing; and last but not least, my partner, Juliet, for all of her tremendous support.

About the Author

Dr. Michael Hewitt was born in South Wales in the United Kingdom. He earned his bachelor of music degree at London University and a master's degree and doctorate at the University of Bangor, where he specialized in musical composition. He is a classically trained musician, a composer, a lecturer, and an author on musical subjects. Working to commission, he writes classical scores as well as soundtracks for various television productions, both at home and abroad. He is currently working as a music technology tutor at Coleg Harlech, North Wales, whose full-time residential adult education courses are run against the backdrop of the beautiful mountains of Snowdonia.

Contents

Chapter 6
Common Values   75

Chapter 7
Producing Basslines   79

Chapter 8
Writing Melodic Leads   99

Chapter 9
Melody, Bass, and Harmony   113

Chapter 10
The Creative Use of FX   123

Chapter 15
Sampling   169

Chapter 16
Control Data   179

Chapter 17
Approaching Structure   185

Chapter 18
Layering and Sequencing   191

Chapter 19
Mixing and Mastering   203

Conclusion   211

Index   213

Introduction

The probable reason that you are reading this book is that you write (or are perhaps intending to write) your own music tracks using software, and you want to get some tips and information on the best way to go about this. You might be extremely knowledgeable about the software that you use, have a good understanding of your own genre, and even have a good basic understanding of music theory. Even given such knowledge, however, this does not necessarily mean that you can write effective music tracks. You need another kind of knowledge on top of all that. That is the knowledge of *composition*, which as far as computer musicians are concerned, is also sometimes misleadingly called *music production*.

Composition as a subject concerns itself with the answers to such questions as: How do I write a good drum track? What is the best way to write a bassline? How do I write a beautiful, soaring melodic lead? How do I write a percussion track? What is the best way to structure my music? The answers to these types of questions all fall under the cover of the blanket term *composition*, and whatever kind of music you write, you will be using composition and compositional techniques at every stage.

A compositional technique is a procedure that you follow to obtain an effective musical result. Knowledge of these techniques is essential for the process of good music writing. Imagine a bricklayer going to build a brick wall without knowledge of the techniques of bricklaying. There are only so many ways to build a sturdy wall effectively with bricks. Without knowledge of what these are, though, the whole process of building a wall would be very random and haphazard, and you probably would not want to pay good money to have a wall such as this built for you. It is exactly the same with music. There are tried-and-true techniques and methods for writing and building up musical material, and these are just as essential for a music producer or composer to know about as the techniques of wall building are for a bricklayer to know.

A person writing his or her own music tracks won't get very far without a clear understanding of musical structure. There are specific ways to organize and structure your musical material that, over a long period of time, have proven themselves to be universally effective. These ways are a type of compositional technique, a method for the organization and arrangement of your musical material. Learning about these different methods as they apply to the different parameters of the music that you are writing is, in effect, learning about the process of musical composition.

Getting the Best out of Your Setup

This book is written primarily for the computer musician—a person who uses computer technology for the purposes of creating new or original musical works. There are numerous types of software that have been developed for this purpose. The software that you choose to use all depends upon the type(s) of music that you are writing. We'll now consider some of the main types of software designed for this purpose.

Score-Writing Programs

One such type of software includes score-writing programs, such as Sibelius, Finale, and NotePad. These programs were originally designed to ease the labor involved for a composer who needed to produce a professional-looking score together with the various separate parts that might be needed for individual performers of the music. I produce such scores, and I used to have to write out the score and all of the separate parts by hand with a fountain pen. For an orchestral piece, the labor involved in this is immense because it is necessary to write up to a hundred separate parts without a single mistake. And the task is made no easier by the fact that some of the parts would have to be transposed, such as the bass clarinet part, which has to be transposed up a major ninth. These days it is so much easier to write the score using a computer program that is capable of automatically producing the different parts, including their appropriate transpositions.

By incorporating MIDI technology, these score-writing programs have now become capable of triggering sounds from an external hardware (or equivalent software) device, such as a synthesizer. In this way it becomes possible for composers not only to write their scores using the appropriate program, but also to gain a preview of what the final work will sound like. This technology has since become supplemented by various plug-ins, which amount to huge sample banks of orchestral sounds that make the sound that much more realistic. Such technology is still in its early days and, as far as I'm concerned, is not yet capable of producing self-sufficient compositions that do not need the original instruments. When such a day does arrive, it is possible that the symphony orchestra might find itself becoming redundant!

1

I usually find that those who use score-writing programs tend to have far greater knowledge of composition than those who don't. This is because to use a score-writing program, you have to be able to read music. Those who have been taught or have learned to read music have often learned music theory on the way. This knowledge often helps a great deal in the process of composition.

Loop-Based Computer Programs

Another proprietary type of software for music-creation purposes includes the various loop-based programs, such as ACID Pro, GarageBand, FruityLoops, and MUSIC 3000. As part of the package, these programs offer large banks of pre-composed copyright-free loops, which the computer musician is free to combine and arrange to produce a final product. Some of them also offer MIDI capabilities, which means it is possible to create and record your own loops. A lot of computer musicians I know started out this way, and through the use of these programs, they acquired at least some skill in terms of arranging loops into a complete track. After a while, though, the novelty of being able to create tracks mostly using loops that somebody else has written often starts to fade, and the musician starts to feel like a bit of a cheat.

Propellerhead Reason

Once they have reached this stage, many such musicians tend to progress to a program such as Propellerhead's Reason. Like the programs mentioned earlier, Reason offers a selection of pre-composed loops (Dr.Rex files), but this is not its major strength. In essence, it offers a rack of VSTs(*Virtual Synthesizer Technology*)—that is, software synthesizers and samplers with which you can compose and record your own material. However, one of its main limitations is that it does not allow the use of any other VSTs you might have on board (such as Absynth, for example). Instead, it offers a closed package consisting of a number of generic devices, including synthesizers, a drum machine, and two excellent samplers. The latter two make up for the lack of audio recording facilities in Reason, which is to say that you have to record your audio using another program and then import it as an audio file into one of the samplers.

The DAW

As perhaps a better and more flexible alternative to Reason, many computer musicians prefer to use one of the major DAWs (*digital audio workstations*) on the market, such as Logic, Cubase, Cakewalk SONAR, Digital Performer, or Pro Tools (see Figure 1.1). These have numerous common features that make them great tools for the computer musician. For a start, they enable the recording and editing of audio material, an essential feature if you want to introduce a live vocal or other instruments into your tracks. They also enable the recording of MIDI data and therefore allow the use of hardware devices, such as synthesizers and drum machines. And to supplement this, they also enable the use of a wide range of VSTs, which includes software synths, drum machines, samplers, and many excellent computer-based simulations of famous and classic hardware devices, such as the Roland 303. A good DAW, therefore, gives musicians a wide range of freedom in the development of their musical projects in that they are capable of combining audio, MIDI, and VSTs into one really effective package.

Figure 1.1   Logic Express Arrange window. Logic Express offers full MIDI capability as well as a wide range of software instruments.

ReWire Technology

Another facility that the DAW offers is ReWire technology, often used with Reason. We have already observed that Reason is limited because it does not allow MIDI or audio recording. This limitation can be easily overcome using ReWire technology, which enables the DAW to control the devices used in Reason through a master/slave relationship. In effect, this means that the Reason devices are completely controlled and operated through the DAW. I know of numerous computer musicians who productively use this type of setup. They write a lot of their material in Reason and then use ReWire to bring that material into their chosen DAW, often Cubase, where they add further elements along with any live audio they want (see Figure 1.2). The track is then mixed in its final form using the DAW and all of the processing effects that it can offer.

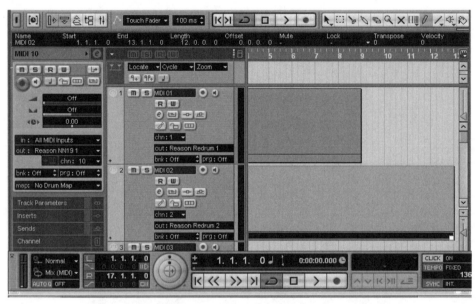

Figure 1.2   Many producers like to work with the sounds of Reason coupled with the processing power of Cubase. This link between the two programs is achieved through ReWire technology.

The DAW as the Heart of the Setup

At the heart of the preferred setup for many of today's computer musicians is the DAW, which through ReWire establishes a direct connection with Reason. Through the MIDI capabilities of the DAW, your rack of hardware synths is ready to feed into the mix, while through the audio applications, your microphones are ready to record any live elements of sound you need. Add to this the vast number of VSTs that you can potentially add to your setup, and you will find that you have total and absolute freedom to develop your music in any way that is required.

Ableton Live

An important alternative option to the DAW for many writers and producers of music is Ableton Live (see Figure 1.3). Ableton fulfills many of the functions of a DAW in that it offers audio, MIDI, ReWire, and VST channels, all of which can be used together and combined. Yet it also has some extra features due to the fact that Ableton was originally designed as a DJing tool that enabled the DJ to import tracks into the program as audio files. As you cue up the tracks, Ableton automatically beat matches them for you. Because this process is a large part of the traditional DJ's job, some DJs felt that this was also a type of cheating.

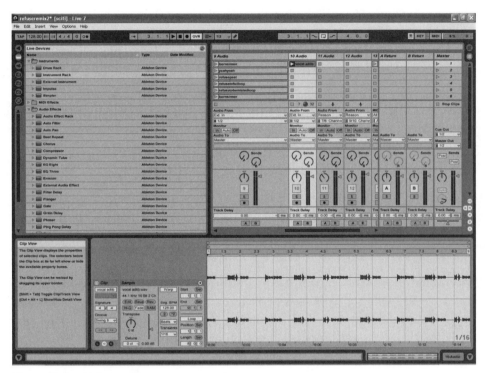

Figure 1.3 Ableton Live.

Yet for the music producer, Ableton offers some remarkable facilities, which in recent years have been used to create some great albums and live sets. A good example is Richie Hawtin's *Transitions*, an album created on Ableton using loops that he ingeniously weaves together from about 150 separate records. Using this kind of facility, Ableton is great for live sets, where it is possible to creatively combine both original and imported material in a live performing situation to create new, fresh, and original works.

Slowly Building Up Your Studio

To purchase an entire studio setup, which includes your chosen DAW together with Reason and any other VSTs that you would like to obtain, can be rather expensive, especially when you add in the costs of decent monitors, a mixer, a suitable MIDI interface, microphones, and other ancillaries. And the valuable option of incorporating hardware synthesizers into your setup makes the total cost even more prohibitive. So, it is probably best to start off with what you can afford and build it up bit by bit. If you like electronica and dance music, a good place to start is with Reason. Although the onboard sound banks can be a bit limited, these are nonetheless supported and supplemented by a huge number of refills that may be free or may come with a charge. The majority of refills cater to particular styles of music, such as the Chemical Synths refill favored by drum and bass writers or the Clubotica refill favored by writers of house and techno music.

If you do get Reason, make sure you also invest in ReCycle, which gives you great ways to chop up loops and create audio slices. Together with ReCycle, you will also need an appropriate WAV editor, such as Sony Creative Software Sound Forge. This enables you to record and edit audio files on your computer, which you can then either turn into loops using ReCycle or import straight into one of Reason's samplers.

The next stage is to get yourself a decent MIDI controller, which is usually a keyboard. Although it has no onboard sounds, this is used to generate MIDI data, such as note on/off messages, which you use to control and record from Reason's devices. This way, you can directly play and record from your keyboard whatever device you have selected.

The next stage in the development of your home studio might be to purchase a DAW or perhaps Ableton Live, depending upon your preferences. Both work with VSTs and offer the facility of ReWire technology, which means that in both cases your compositional options are greatly expanded. Indeed, from this point on you can start to add in various VSTs as you can afford them. Each VST that you purchase will give you a broader potential spectrum of expression. The alternative to VSTs at this stage is a decent hardware synth, such as a Korg Triton or a Roland Fantom-X. I personally love the sound of a good hardware synth, and I would never be without one. But that is purely my preference. The disadvantage of a good hardware synth is the sheer price—they can cost as much as your computer and all of your software programs put together!

Conclusion

The concern of this chapter has been the type of setup that you work with. We've discussed the different types of software you might be using and the way in which some types of software are capable of working with others, such as ReWire technology. The process of getting to know that software and finding out what it is capable of doing will take you many hours of exploring and experimenting. Yet whatever that software is, you should always remember that in the end, the software is just a tool. It is a tool that has been devised to enable you to create and produce your own music. Once you have learned to use that tool, the next area to consider is the music that you will be writing with it. In many ways, this is not software dependent. Consequently, it is possible to write a really good drum and bass track using any one of a number of different music software programs. This shows us that behind the writing of drum and bass—or indeed, any other type of music—there is a particular knowledge needed, in addition to the knowledge required to operate your software. This is the knowledge of music production and composition, which is the subject of this book.

In covering this subject I am going to assume that you have some kind of knowledge of at least basic music theory. If you do not, I recommend that you acquire this knowledge as soon as possible. All of the knowledge you will require in this area can be obtained in my book *Music Theory for Computer Musicians* (Course Technology PTR, 2008).

When considering music composition and production, the obvious question that arises is where to start. Although it might seem logical to jump straight in with the technicalities of musical production, I find that the best place to start the study of music composition and production is with a keen study of genre—that is, the type of music being produced. The reason why is that producing music successfully within a particular genre requires a precise knowledge of the techniques used to compose and produce it. Therefore, if you intend to write music within a particular genre, your first concern must be to familiarize yourself with that genre and the various techniques and methods used to write it. For this reason, the concern of the next chapter will be genres of music.

2 Knowing Your Genre

There is a great range of different styles of music available to the consumer today. These are normally classified by their genre. Examples of different genres are hip-hop, classical, folk, dance, jazz, and so on. Within a given genre, there are also numerous subgenres. Like branches growing out from the trunk of a tree, these become ever more diverse. Therefore, if a person informs you that he likes trance, this is not really enough information to indicate exactly what his musical preferences are. The next question is what type of trance: hard, melodic, psychedelic, Euro, symphonic, euphoric, death, pop, ambient, nu, and so on? And these are just some of the options within one genre, which itself is a subgenre of dance music. See Figure 2.1.

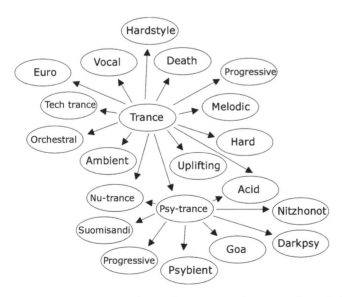

Figure 2.1 Trance and its subgenres. Each genre of music has numerous subgenres. To write successfully in a particular style, you need to hone in on the precise techniques used to create and produce it.

The Implications of Genre

As a computer musician, you are intending to write your own music. Whatever music you write, it will have a genre. I often hear people, especially computer musicians, remark that they don't really like the word *genre* and that it is not productive to label and pigeonhole music in this way. In many ways this is true, because the idea of genre can act as some kind of restriction on the computer musician's creative freedom. Ideally, the computer musician should be free to write whatever kind of music occurs to him, rather than being bound in some way by the preconceptions that belong with genre. Yet even this attitude itself intimates a particular genre, because music written in this way is usually called *experimental*. Another term for it is *progressive*, in that the music aims to push the boundaries that we associate with the word *genre*. So whichever way you look at it, the genre of the music does not go away.

Of course, we should not forget that genre is essentially a very convenient label. The primary convenience is a purely commercial one. If you write and sell a track to a publishing company, they are going to want to market it. To market it, they have to make sure the track reaches the intended buyer. To do so, the music has to fit into a niche where it can be placed and sold and where the buyer can find it. As a consumer of music, when you access an online record store to download music, the first thing you look for is your chosen genre. If you are into house music, you don't bother looking through the heavy-metal sections. This categorization of music saves you an awful lot of time because you don't need to plow through thousands of tracks belonging to every possible genre. So the convenient label that we call *genre* is also useful for you. It fast-tracks you straight to the kind of music that you are looking for.

For people wishing to write their own music, the genre also serves another very important purpose. Each type of genre has important precedents by which it is generally defined. For example, it is difficult to think of acid house without Josh Wink's seminal track "Higher State of Conscious" coming to mind. In academic terms, tracks of this sort represent the canon by which a particular genre is defined. Consequently, if you are writing within a particular genre, you cannot avoid the fact that your music will be judged and listened to in terms of how it measures up against that canon.

Genre and Compositional Technique

As a producer of your own music, this leads to two important considerations. First, you need to learn both the compositional techniques and the features of style associated with that canon. Second, you need to consider how you can contribute something new to that genre. The latter is essential. It is clearly not enough just to imitate the sound that is out there already. By the time it gets to the marketplace—assuming that it even does—it will already have fallen far behind the current progressions and innovations going on within that particular genre.

To write within a given genre, then, you first need to know the tracks that most clearly define the genre. And by *know*, I mean you need to have completely mastered all of the techniques and tricks that were used to write the music. Once you've gotten that far, you then need to think about how to shape and mold that genre to your own purposes, how to make it yours, how to infuse it with your own voice, and how to put your own signature upon it. Madonna did this with the dying genre of disco. She took all of the features of the original genre and turned them to her own creative purposes. In doing so, she turned a floundering genre on its last legs into a unique feature of her own voice.

Once you know the kind of genre(s) in which you want to write, you are then in a really useful position of knowing what you need to learn to be able do it successfully. Each type of genre demands a particular knowledge of compositional and production techniques that belong with it. And generally, it is true that the techniques applicable to one genre are not always applicable to another. If you write drum and bass, your prime focus has to be on learning how to write and produce those amazing drum tracks and killer bass lines that define the genre. The knowledge you acquire to do this is not generally transferable to other genres—unless you are trying to fuse together elements of different genres.

A New Way of Listening to Music

Once you know the genres of music that you want to write, you need to start listening to the music you love in a completely different way. The sooner you can get a handle on this, the better. We usually listen to music in a passive way, and the wizardry and expertise of the writer directly affects us at that level. We hear a really amazing solo and emotionally respond to it. However, once you have decided to start writing your own music, you have to develop an altogether new way of listening to music. This new method indirectly takes into account all of the music that you will ever encounter, irrespective of its genre. As a producer of your own music, you need to know all about the techniques used to write it. Once you have mastered these techniques, like a skillful performer you can then infuse the music with your own feeling, style, and flair.

To get a handle on these techniques, you need to start listening to music in a more inquisitive way. You need to constantly ask questions such as: How was that bass line written? What is that kick drum pattern? What is the quality of that snare? Is the texture of the music wet or dry? How has the writer produced that distinctive, soaring lead? What kind of reverb is on that amazing vocal? How did the writer produce that rippling arpeggio in the piano part? What chords were used in that amazing chord progression?

This essentially active, more analytical process of listening can get quite technical. It is comparable to the difference between, say, an ordinary person entering a room and a forensic scientist on an important case entering the same room. The attentiveness, alertness, and scrutiny of the forensic scientist would leave the ordinary person far behind. You are that forensic scientist, and the music you listen to is the room being examined.

I have known people who produce their own music who find it really useful to sit down with a pen and paper in front of them, put on their favorite track, and then listen to it over and over again, slowly and meticulously charting out bar by bar everything that happens in the track. By doing this they gain a huge amount of information about how their favorite artists develop and organize their musical material. I'll discuss this in more detail in Chapter 17, "Approaching Structure."

Open Your Mind to Other Genres

Don't just listen to the music of your own genre in this very attentive way. Start listening to every type of music that you come across in exactly the same way. Even if you personally don't like the music of a particular genre, if you come across it and it happens to be playing, listen attentively to it. Every piece of music that you encounter is absolutely brimming with valuable lessons you can learn. Behind that musical production are probably many years of experience and learning about musical composition and production. And even if through attentive listening you only learn a new way of processing your hi-hats, that is still a valuable lesson you can use to improve your own music writing.

Conclusion

This chapter talked about the practical and commercial necessity for genre and the importance of computer musicians having a clear idea of the genre(s) of music they are interested in writing. We discussed the importance of knowing the canon by which a genre is defined, together with the necessity for music producers to master the compositional and production techniques belonging to that canon. Having mastered these, producers of their own music will then be in a position to contribute something new to that genre. This chapter also pointed to the importance of learning how to listen to music in a new way. Rather than just passively listening to music, would-be writers of their own music need to listen to it actively, paying great attention to every detail and asking themselves how the various elements of a track were actually written and produced.

Having discussed the importance of genre, we are now in a position to consider the technicalities of writing a musical project. To compose a complete project from beginning to end involves many separate processes, which include laying down of the rhythm track, the bass, the lead, any fills, the vocal, and so on. Because these elements are always assigned their own particular sequencer track(s), they have to be laid down in a particular order. The exact order in which they are laid down is, of course, up to you and your own particular preferences. Most computer musicians, however, tend to lay down the drum track first. This is because the drum track provides a clear sense of time and rhythm over which the other parts can then be laid down. For this reason, the most logical place with which to begin a study of the technicalities of music production is the drum track itself. This will provide the topic for the next chapter.

3 Rhythm and Drum Programming

Chapter 2 discussed the importance of having a good general knowledge of your own particular genre(s). In this and subsequent chapters, we will become much more specific and will begin to start focusing on particular areas of music production. One of the most important of these areas is rhythm and drum programming. The importance of this area cannot be underestimated. This is because in one way or another, issues of drum programming have a direct relevance to virtually all known styles of modern computer-generated music tracks.

It is also an important place to start your study of musical production simply because, when creating a complete musical project, many people—including myself—like to put down a beat first. This beat not only imparts a sense of time and measure to the composition, but it also creates an initial groove and sense of style that can provide a strong stimulus for the music production process.

The nature and type of beat laid down will of course depend upon the precise style of music being written. However, on occasion you might have a really great musical idea that comes to you without a beat. In such cases the beat is then composed and laid down after the tune. Yet regardless of the order in which these elements are composed, the fact remains that to be able to produce professional-sounding tracks, you need to have the ability to write an effective drum track in the first place.

Unfortunately, writing a good drum track is, and always has been, one of the great challenges for many computer musicians. This is because although the drums are a really important element, for much of today's music producing an effective drum track on the computer from scratch can prove to be an extremely difficult task. One of the most popular solutions to this problem is to use pre-composed drum loops obtained from various sources.

Using Pre-Composed Drum Loops

Most music-writing software programs offer a wide selection of pre-composed drum loops. Therefore, to create an instant drum track, all you need to do is audition and select a suitable pattern and paste it into the chosen track. To supplement this process, there are also many CDs on the market that offer thousands of drum patterns of different styles, all ready and waiting for you to simply import them into your track. Creating a drum track could never be easier.

Another option in this category—although it requires slightly more effort—is to download MIDI files of drum tracks from the Internet. Just Google "free MIDI files" and you will find literally hundreds of GM (*General MIDI*) files of drum patterns, which, due to their GM format, can be appropriately realized on any MIDI-compatible drum kit.

Given this available wealth of material, all there and ready for use, why bother even trying to write your own drum track? After all, it is the tune people like and respond to, isn't it? Really, this comes down to a matter of choice, integrity, and of course the kind of music you want to write. In some styles of music—such as drum and bass, where the drums are such a vital element, or tribal house and tribal techno, where the drums virtually are the music—the drum track is such a key feature that if you *did* use precomposed loops, it contradicts the point of even trying to write the music in the first place. This is comparable to showing an exhibit of painting by numbers that you have done and calling yourself an artist!

Although I do know people who started out using drum loops, it was not long before their desire for personal artistic expression led them to the necessity and inevitability of writing their own drum tracks. And once you have reached this point, this is where the learning curve to write an effective and realistic drum track begins.

Studying a Real Drum Kit

When you are learning to write drum tracks, there is really only one place to start, and that is to look at a real drum kit. Now, some people might argue with this and say they write techno, and that doesn't use real drums. However, they will eventually discover that initially, at least, musical style is irrelevant, simply because all drum programming is built upon the initial practices and foundations of a drummer playing a proper acoustic drum kit. This is where the process of drumming begins, and all of the essential features and foundations of today's drum programming are there in embryonic form. Therefore, to gain a secure foundation in drum programming, it is necessary to start at the logical place—a drum kit being played by a drummer! Figure 3.1 shows an example of such a drum kit.

This particular kit has 13 pieces. The largest drum that you can see in the foreground of the picture is the bass drum, more commonly known as the *kick drum*—a drum that is played with a beater made of felt, played with a foot pedal. Because it is played with the foot, the kick drum does not lend itself to fast, intricate patterns, although this does

Figure 3.1 An acoustic drum kit.

become more feasible with a double-pedal, which allows both feet to be used. Alternatively, for these purposes a drummer might even use two kicks.

To the back right of the kit, you can see the snare drum, which is usually played with wooden sticks (or sometimes brushes). It has a much brighter and more piercing sound than the bass drum. Snare drums have a set of metal coils at the bottom of the head that vibrate when the drum is struck, producing that characteristic snare-drum sound. These coils can be removed if you want to produce a less rattling sound.

You can obtain great variations of tone by hitting the drumhead in different places and with differing degrees of force. Struck very gently, the snare effect is more predominant. I am sure you have heard this in those gentle rolls played by military bands. When the head is hit much harder, you'll hear a fuller sound with a very strong sense of attack to it. A well-known effect on the snare drum is the rimshot, which involves hitting the metal rim of the drum to produce a sharp cracking sound. You can play other drums in this way as well.

To the right of the drum kit (as pictured), you can see the hi-hats, which consist of two horizontal cymbals facing opposite each other, attached to a stand at the bottom of which is a pedal. When the pedal is pressed, the two cymbals separate. This is called the *open hi-hat*, and when struck by a stick, it produces a very resonant cymbal sound compared to that of the closed hi-hat. When the pedal is released into its normal position, the hi-hat is said to be *closed*, and when struck, it produces a much shorter, crisper metallic sound. Hi-hat parts are characteristically a mixture of both open and closed hi-hat sounds.

Toward the front of the drum kit, you can see four drums of varying sizes. These are the toms, and because they are different sizes, they necessarily produce notes of different pitches, with the larger toms producing the deeper tom sounds. Toms are most often used for fills found at the end of drum phrases, and it is a common effect for a drummer to start with the smallest tom and then accelerate the pace as he gradually works his way down through the range.

At the end of such fills, a crash cymbal is often played to announce the beginning of a new section or phrase of music. The drum kit in Figure 3.1 has numerous cymbals, the most obvious being the crash and the ride cymbals. As its name suggests, the crash produces a full-on crashing cymbal sound. In addition to being used at the end of fills, it can also be used in softer contexts to punctuate and bring emphasis to certain beats of the bass drum.

I once heard an amazing use of crash cymbals where the crash was hit hard with the knuckles and then a microphone moved around in circles beneath it as the sound faded away. This produced the most unearthly resonating sound, which goes to show that you should not always think inside the box when it comes to using traditional instruments.

The ride cymbals, which you might recognize from their use in jazz drumming, have a much softer and more resonant bell-like cymbal sound. They are often used with (or as a substitute for) the regular tap-tap-tap of the hi-hats. Sometimes accessories are used as a part of the drum kit, a favorite accessory being the cowbell, which is often used in alternation with the hi-hat to produce some really interesting patterns. Further accessories, such as congas, the dumbek, and other exotic types of percussion instruments are often played by separate players. These will be discussed in Chapter 4, "Writing for Percussion."

To Learn about Drumming, Watch a Drummer

Once you understand a drum kit so that you can picture it clearly in your mind's eye, the next stage is to watch some seasoned drummers at work. You can learn a huge amount about drum programming by watching a good drummer. The most obvious thing to watch out for is how the drummer uses the sticks.

For starters, a drummer is not an octopus, although I imagine an octopus really would make a good drummer! The player only has two sticks to handle. I know this is obvious, but the number of times where I have seen people programming drum tracks that are totally unplayable by a drummer is quite surprising. When writing drum tracks on a computer, you might think it's unnecessary to write a playable drum track. But the important point here is that a playable drum track sounds much more realistic. It has clarity, a clear definition, and rhythmic articulation *because* the ride cymbal (for example) is not banging away at the same time as the hi-hat, the snare, and the cowbell!

If you have never played the drums, try it if you get the opportunity—you will learn a lot this way as well. You will get at least some kind of an idea of what two hands and a foot can do. Ideally, while writing your drum tracks—especially those related to acoustic types of drum kit—you should picture in your mind how a drummer would play it. And if you think this sounds difficult, count your blessings, because a composer for a symphony orchestra must develop the ability to do this for every single instrument being written for.

Drum Machines

After you have studied the makeup of a conventional drum kit and spent some time watching drummers at work, you will be in a good position to make sensible use of a synthesized or sampled drum kit. By this I mean a drum kit that is provided by a hardware/software drum machine or sampler. Whether you use hardware or software is a matter of personal choice.

Hardware Drum Machines

Hardware drum machines come in all shapes and sizes. Popular ones today are the Roland Boss DR-880, the Akai XR20, and the Alesis SR18. Most drum machines consist of a series of touch-sensitive pads arranged in rows, with each pad triggering a particular drum sample or synthesized drum sound. The pads themselves have programmable parameters that often include the directional pan, the pitch of the drum sound, and fine tuning options. And you can apply various insert FX, such as delay, reverb, and flanging, to each of these sounds.

All drum machines come with a good selection of generic types of drum kits to suit your needs. They also usually provide selections of sampled beat-box noises (the human voice imitating drum sounds), vocal hits, and even bass sounds. In terms of the latter, the drum pads will typically convert to a chromatic range of keys so that you can compose a bassline over your drum pattern. In this respect, a good drum machine provides you with everything you need to lay down a basic rhythm. Additionally, you can import drum sounds and other samples, enabling you to create your own drum kits.

Drum machines allow you to record in real time—in other words, to play the pads as if they were drums and record your performance. Otherwise, you can sequence patterns step by step. The skill with which drum machines can be played these days can be quite staggering. Perhaps you have seen videos on YouTube of performers playing the most incredibly intricate and complex patterns. Of course, to reach this level of skill takes an awful lot of practice, and sometimes I wonder why the person concerned has not actually taken up the drums, given the amount of time he has spent on the drum machine.

Most hardware synthesizers and samplers offer a wide range of different types of drum kits. The playing environment is different here because you are using a piano keyboard to trigger the drum samples. And on a synthesizer/sampler, each kit can have many separate samples. With so many samples to choose from, the prospect of writing an effective drum pattern can be extremely daunting. Figure 3.2 shows a General MIDI standard drum kit.

A novice attempting to write a drum track might look at this huge keyboard range of drum sounds and gasp, "Where do I begin?" Simple—by watching a live drummer playing a drum kit. This will impart a strong sense of priorities in terms of the drum sounds available to create a drum track.

Software Drum Machines

If you do not use hardware in your setup, then you will be limited to the use of software drum machines and samplers. A good example is Redrum, the drum machine that comes with Propellerhead's Reason. This particular drum machine is a software emulation in the style of some of the older classic drum machines, such as the Roland 808/909. It has 16 buttons for programming and sequencing step patterns and 10 separate channels into which samples can be loaded.

The most common file formats for samples are .wav for Windows-based applications and .aiff for Mac-based applications. Because Redrum accepts both .wav and .aiff format files, it is remarkably easy to change any of the drum sounds. And of course, you do not need to be limited to drum sounds. Redrum will play any kind of suitable audio file, such as excerpts of speech, for example.

Another type of software drum machine is Logic's Ultrabeat drum synthesizer (see Figure 3.3). This great little machine enables precise control of the various parameters of each drum sound.

Functional Elements of Drum Programming: The Kick and the Snare

When you are first attempting to write drum tracks, it is very easy to create a chaotic mess of beats. Although you might be proud of this as a first attempt, you will soon realize that the result has very little musical value. Save yourself an enormous amount of time and follow this advice: When creating a drum track, the most important functional elements are generally the kick and the snare.

If you can grasp this essential concept, you will already be well on your way to producing effective and realistic drum patterns. This is because doing so shows an important

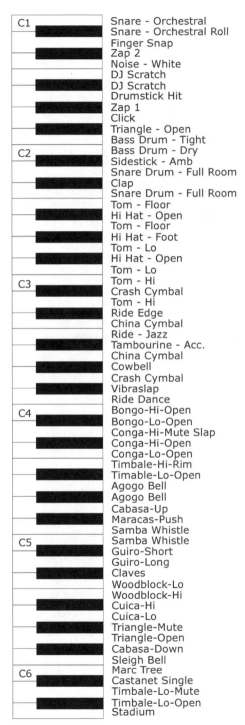

Snare - Orchestral
Snare - Orchestral Roll
Finger Snap
Zap 2
Noise - White
DJ Scratch
DJ Scratch
Drumstick Hit
Zap 1
Click
Triangle - Open
Bass Drum - Tight
Bass Drum - Dry
Sidestick - Amb
Snare Drum - Full Room
Clap
Snare Drum - Full Room
Tom - Floor
Hi Hat - Open
Tom - Floor
Hi Hat - Foot
Tom - Lo
Hi Hat - Open
Tom - Lo
Tom - Hi
Crash Cymbal
Tom - Hi
Ride Edge
China Cymbal
Ride - Jazz
Tambourine - Acc.
China Cymbal
Cowbell
Crash Cymbal
Vibraslap
Ride Dance
Bongo-Hi-Open
Bongo-Lo-Open
Conga-Hi-Mute Slap
Conga-Hi-Open
Conga-Lo-Open
Timbale-Hi-Rim
Timable-Lo-Open
Agogo Bell
Agogo Bell
Cabasa-Up
Maracas-Push
Samba Whistle
Samba Whistle
Guiro-Short
Guiro-Long
Claves
Woodblock-Lo
Woodblock-Hi
Cuica-Hi
Cuica-Lo
Triangle-Mute
Triangle-Open
Cabasa-Down
Sleigh Bell
Marc Tree
Castanet Single
Timbale-Lo-Mute
Timbale-Lo-Open
Stadium

Figure 3.2   General MIDI standard drum kit.

Figure 3.3 Logic's Ultrabeat drum machine.

sense of priority. When looking at a sampled drum kit, which may include more than 100 sounds, one of the first priorities is to find a kick drum sound that you want, together with a suitable snare drum. Once you have selected these, you will have in your possession the two most important functional elements of a workable drum pattern.

Between them, the kick and the snare provide the essential rhythm upon which an entire drum pattern is based. They represent the backbone of the drum pattern, the structural core from which it is built. You can easily confirm this by watching any seasoned drummer at work. Observe that the downbeats—Beats 1 and 3—are nearly always provided by the bass drum, while the snare usually offers a contrast on the so-called backbeat— Beats 2 and 4. This custom of the backbeat stems from the early days of rock drumming, but it is so effective that it has since become a more or less universal feature of many other styles of drumming. An exception to this is perhaps in reggae, which often uses the snare on Beat 3.

Viewing this general pattern as a repetitive cycle in time, we could represent it as a diagram like the one shown in Figure 3.4.

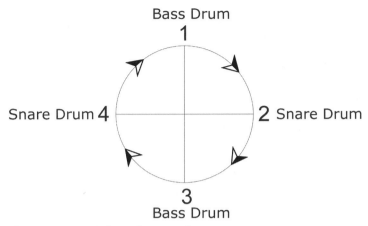

Figure 3.4 Basic bass drum and snare pattern.

Looking at the diagram in Figure 3.4, you will soon realize that drum playing—in particular the bass-snare interaction—has a strong sense of polarity about it. The bass drum beats orient themselves along a north-south axis, and the snare on an east-west axis. Another useful way of looking at this polarity is in terms of questions and answers. The bass drum sound is like a question—"How are you today?"—while the snare drum sound is like an answer to that question—"I am fine, thank you." Notice that both are reliant upon each other for their mutual effect: The snare is the reaction or response to the kick, which is the action. Kick is to snare as action is to response.

Knowing this basic fact allows you to break down the process of writing a drum pattern into a number of basic steps. First, find a kick and snare that suit your purposes. Second, compose your kick-snare pattern. The pattern in Figure 3.4—which simply goes Beat 1 – kick, Beat 2 – snare, Beat 3 – kick, Beat 4 – snare—is one of the most basic patterns that it is possible to create. But don't necessarily dismiss it because of its simplicity. It was used to great effect in Black Sabbath's "Paranoid."

Kick-Snare Patterns

Over the years a number of important kick-snare patterns have proved themselves invaluable to drummers and music producers alike. Naturally, these range from the simpler ones to the more complex. I recommend that you experiment with some of the simpler variations because these tend to be the ones that are used over and over again. Now, you might say that you would like to do something original with your drums. That is great, but first learn the basics. Then you will be in an excellent position to come up with a new variation.

The simplest kick-snare pattern I have heard is the one Phil Collins uses in the song "In the Air Tonight." This is identical to the pattern mentioned a moment ago, except that the kick is missing on Beat 3. It looks like what you see in Figure 3.5.

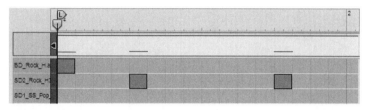

Figure 3.5   Kick-snare pattern 1 (Track 1 on the audio CD).

If you were step-sequencing this pattern on a drum machine with a resolution of sixteenths, it would appear like what you see in Figure 3.6.

	1				5				9				13			
Kick	X															
Snare					X								X			

Figure 3.6   Kick-snare pattern 1.

Another common pattern is where the kick takes the two eighths on Beat 3 (see Figure 3.7).

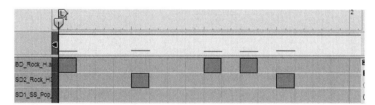

Figure 3.7   Kick-snare pattern 2 (Track 2 on the audio CD).

This pattern can be heard in Coldplay's "My Frustration" and parts of Bon Jovi's "It's My Life" (Verse 1). And it is a pattern that would be step-sequenced as shown in Figure 3.8.

	1				5				9				13			
Kick	X								X		X					
Snare					X								X			

Figure 3.8   Kick-snare pattern 2.

A variation of this pattern is to omit the kick on Beat 3, as occurs in Moby's song, "Bodyrock." See Figure 3.9.

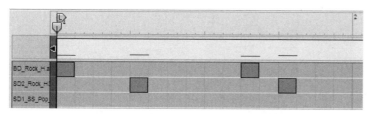

Figure 3.9 Kick-snare pattern 3 (Track 3 on the audio CD).

This pattern can be step-sequenced as shown in Figure 3.10.

	1				5				9				13			
Kick	X								X							
Snare					X								X			

Figure 3.10 Kick-snare pattern 3.

Yet another variant is to bring the kick back from Beat 3 by an eighth, as shown in Figure 3.11.

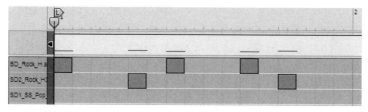

Figure 3.11 Kick-snare pattern 4 (Track 4 on the audio CD).

This pattern (and other variants) is used at times in Nirvana's "Come As You Are." It is also very popular in drum and bass, where an extra snare hit is often put on Step 15. Step-sequenced, this pattern would be programmed as you see in Figure 3.12.

	1				5				9				13			
Kick	X				X				X							
Snare					X								X			

Figure 3.12 Kick-snare pattern 4.

The kick-snare pattern in Figure 3.13 is extremely popular in hip-hop styles, although it has been used elsewhere (for example, in "Monkey Wrench" by The Foo Fighters).

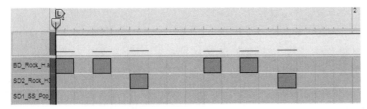

Figure 3.13   Kick-snare pattern 5 (Track 5 on the audio CD).

This pattern would be step-sequenced into a drum machine as you see in Figure 3.14.

1				5				9				13			
X	X							X	X						
			X									X			

Figure 3.14   Kick-snare pattern 5.

In this section I've represented a small selection of some of the simplest one-bar kick-snare patterns in common time (four beats to the bar). Such time-honored patterns represent a good starting point for the exploration of drum programming. Once you have learned to create your own simple kick-snare patterns, you can go on to start composing more intricate patterns or patterns that are longer than a single bar.

Drummers like to mix it up when it comes to kick-snare patterns so that the drumming doesn't become too predictable. You can also experiment with other time signatures. For example, listen to the drums in Pink Floyd's "Money," a song in septuple meter (seven beats to the bar).

An excellent way to come up with core kick-snare patterns is to beat-box them, assigning the sound "boom" to the kick and "tsh" to the snare. The "boom" and "tsh" are words that try to describe my vocalizations of these sounds. You might have your own. As you might have guessed, by beat-box I mean imitating the drum sounds with your voice. It is no coincidence that many cultures teach percussion through the vocalization of drum sounds in this way, the logic being that if you can learn to vocalize a drum pattern, it will be a lot easier when you actually try to play it. Beat-boxing a pattern also ensures that you keep it simple: If you can't beat-box a kick-snare pattern, it is probably not a very good one anyway.

Two-, Four-, and Eight-Bar Extensions

Notice that all of the aforementioned patterns are only one bar long. Feasibly, you can use one-bar drum patterns, but after a while they start to sound mechanical and repetitive. Many drum patterns are of two-, four-, and eight-bar lengths.

The reason that such lengths for drum patterns are so popular is all to do with our innate love of balance and symmetry. In a two-bar drum pattern, the second bar acts as an answer or a response to the first bar. In this way, the two complement one another to create a balanced unit. The second bar characteristically has some kind of variation in it that makes it different from the first bar. In a four-bar drum pattern, Bars 3 and 4 act as an answer or response to Bars 1 and 2. So the second set of two bars will also have some kind of variation. And the same applies to eight-bar drum patterns, which are generally divisible into two sets of four bars each, with the second set answering the first set. As a diagram, this process could be represented as shown in Figure 3.15.

Figure 3.15 Relationship between two-, four-, and eight-bar drum patterns.

So how does this apply in practice? This question can be answered by looking at the hip-hop beat in Figure 3.11. This pattern can be extended over two bars by copying and pasting Bar 1 to Bar 2 and then adding a secondary hit on the kick in Bar 2. This sets it apart from Bar 1 and turns it into a complete two-bar pattern, as shown in Figure 3.16.

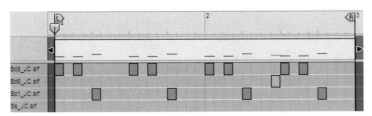

Figure 3.16 Two-bar hip-hop kick-snare pattern (Track 6 on the audio CD).

Secondary hits are usually softer and less prominent than the primary hits that set down the basic beat. They are termed *secondary* because it is their job to add variation, interest, and spice to the basic or primary beat. Usually, secondary hits can be made less prominent by altering the velocity of the hit. Yet when a real drummer plays a drum more softly, there are also tonal changes in the sound. Reducing the velocity of a sample does not account for these. For this reason, it is advisable to put secondary hits on their own channel, as you can see in Figure 3.16. In this way, both their volume and their timbre can be modified to your satisfaction. One way of modifying such hits is to alter the sample start time in order to reduce their attack. Another is to use a sample from the same drum, but recorded at a lower volume. Good professional banks of drum samples often provide these for you.

The two-bar pattern given in Figure 3.16 can then be converted into a four-bar pattern in a similar way. Copy and paste Bars 1 and 2 to Bars 3 and 4, and then in Bar 4, introduce some further variations through the use of secondary hits on either the kick or the snare. You can see one solution in Figure 3.17.

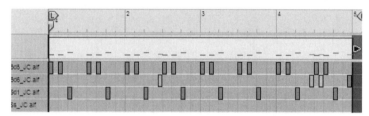

Figure 3.17 Four-bar hip-hop kick-snare pattern (Track 7 on the audio CD).

You now have a four-bar kick-snare pattern suitable for copying and pasting wherever needed. But before you do this, there is another vital element of drum programming to consider—the ride.

The Ride

Between them, the kick and the snare define the two most important functional elements of the drum pattern. A third functional element, called the *ride*, is a regularly spaced hit that gives the drum pattern a sense of continuity and motion. The ride element is most often provided by the hi-hats, although as an alternative, the ride cymbal can also be used either in conjunction with the hi-hats or all on its own. In other contexts, a tambourine, maracas, or a shaker can do the same job. The important feature of the ride element is that it provides that vital sense of continuity and motion.

The ride element can be placed on the quarters, eighths, or sixteenths. Placed on the quarters, the ride can add emphasis to the primary hits, a common technique used in dance music. In most styles of music, the ride element tends to occur on the eighths or the sixteenths. The choice of whether to use eighths or sixteenths all depends upon the type of drum track you want. Eighths give a nice flowing sense to the drums. Sixteenths are more intricate and give a greater sense of pace, motion, and energy.

As is the case with the kick and the snare, secondary hits can be used within the ride element to give the drum pattern more variety, interest, and definition. In the case of a ride on the eighths, these are decorative sixteenths, while in the case of a ride on the sixteenths, these are decorative thirty-seconds. The latter are often used in drum and bass on the last beat to give that exciting sense of rolling motion into the next bar.

In the pattern in Figure 3.18, simple eighths are used, and the last eighth is an open (as opposed to a closed) hi-hat.

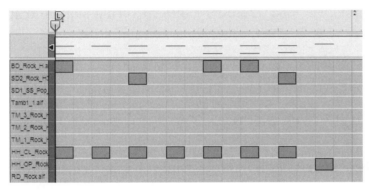

Figure 3.18 Kick-snare pattern 2 with hi-hat eighths (Track 8 on the audio CD).

When using a mixture of open and closed hi-hats, remember that as soon as the hats are closed after an open hi-hat hit, the sound shuts off. On the Redrum drum machine in Reason, this effect is emulated using Channels 8 and 9 exclusive. When the Channels 8 and 9 exclusive button is pressed, the closed hi-hat will function as a cut-off for the open hi-hat. You can see this button on the bottom left of the Redrum device in Figure 3.19.

Figure 3.19 Redrum Channel 8 and 9 exclusive function.

If you are using a sampler, it might be necessary to modify either the loop or the note length in order to emulate this effect of shutoff. Placing the open hi-hat in the ride is a matter of artistic choice. If you do not have much experience with this, then to find the best places for it, lay down the ride in closed hi-hats first and then experiment with substituting a given closed hi-hat hit for an open hi-hat. You will soon discover those points where it works well against the kick-snare pattern.

Your job of writing a drum track is made much easier once you understand that a drum pattern consists of just three basic functional elements: the kick and snare, which define the basic rhythm, and the ride, which is used to impart motion and continuity to that rhythm. Composing a drum pattern is therefore a simple three-step process.

1. Create a working kick-snare rhythm.

2. Add a suitable ride element either on the eighths or the sixteenths.

3. Introduce your secondary hits in order to extend the pattern and give it variety and interest.

It is that simple, and this is where the art of drum programming begins to take off.

Quantization

If you have been recording your drums using a keyboard to trigger the drum samples, you might need to quantize them. You might have read that it is a mistake to quantize your drums, because this leads to a mechanical and rigid sound. In some respects this is true, so quantize the elements of your drum track selectively. Make sure that the kick is dead on the first beat of the bar and that the ride sounds fairly even. But even if you quantize the whole pattern, there is no need to worry, because there are specific techniques (which you have yet to apply) that bring a sense of natural realism to your drums. The first of these techniques is swing.

Swing

Swing is an extremely common feature of drum patterns of all styles, although it is not always rigidly used. Some patterns work best with swing; others work better without it. A drum pattern played without swing is called *straight*. Your choice of whether to use swing depends upon the kind of feel and groove you want to create. It will be well worth your time to seek out a drummer who will demonstrate swing for you.

Swing is the natural effect that occurs when the weaker beats of the rhythm are delayed slightly. By this I mean the off beats—Beats 2, 4, 6, and 8 if applied to eighths, and Beats 2, 4, 6, 8, 10, 12, 14, and 16 when applied to sixteenths. In Figure 3.20, you can see a diagram of swing being applied to the sixteenths. The first sixteenth of any pair is longer in duration, while the second sixteenth is correspondingly shorter and therefore occurs later.

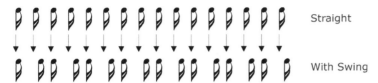

Figure 3.20   Straight and swing sixteenths.

Most drum machines have a swing control that lets you determine how much swing is applied. And most sequencers have swing options that are often included within either the quantization or the Groove menu. The degree of swing offered can range from a marginal amount, where the off beat is only slightly delayed, up to the full range of triplets. In Cubase you can set the degree of swing within the Quantize Setup. In Figure 3.21, it has been set to 25%.

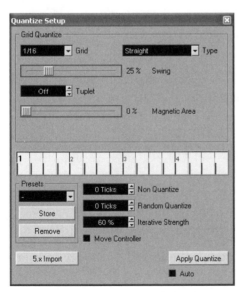

Figure 3.21   The 25% Swing setting in Cubase's Quantize Setup dialog box.

The amount of swing to use is based mostly on the feel of the drum track rather than any particular rule, which means that it is a matter of careful experimentation until you get the feel just right. The example in Figure 3.22 uses swing on the sixteenths.

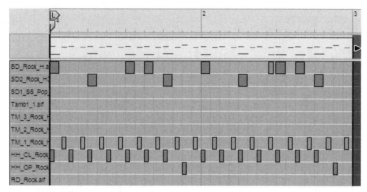

Figure 3.22 Swing applied to ride sixteenths (Track 9 on the audio CD).

Creating Natural Velocity Curves

Another way to create a sense of natural realism within a drum track is to use variations in the velocity—that is, the relative volume or intensity of individual drum hits. If you can imagine a real drummer playing, it will be obvious that aside from deliberate changes in the relative volume of drum hits, it is doubtful that every hit that is intended to be of the same volume actually will be. There will always be a slight plus or minus either way. When we listen to the drums we expect this, and it gives the drumming a sense of interest and vitality.

Composing for drums using a drum machine feasibly enables you to correct this variation in the velocity of the notes played in a live situation. But in fact it would be a grave mistake to do so. There is nothing worse than the mechanical rat-tat-tat of hi-hats all being pumped out at the same velocity. This makes the hi-hat part sound like a typing pool. So if you want your drum programming to have a sense of realism, life, interest, and intensity, you need to adjust the velocity of each drum hit so that together they reflect what you might get from real drumming. Immediately, this would apply, for example, to the strong and weak parts of the bar, the strong parts of the bar normally being on the odd numbered beats, the weak on the even numbers.

In terms of your ride patterns, therefore, you would tend to reduce the velocity of every other hit—that is, all of the hits that fall on the even-numbered sixteenths. Having done so, you would then insert an element of randomness, a plus or minus either way in order to give each hit an individual value. All of this makes the drum pattern sound a lot more natural.

If you are using the same drum for your secondary hits as for your primary hits, you would also have to reduce the velocity on these. What you are looking for is a nice, natural-sounding velocity curve, in which each hit has its own value within the velocity zone that it would normally occupy. I would suggest getting your velocity curve just right from the very first bar. Otherwise, when you have finished your track, you'll need to go through it all in painstaking detail. Although it is not necessary to extend this randomization of velocities beyond, say, a four- or eight-bar pattern, which is then copied and pasted where it is required, you can nonetheless make the entire drum track sound more natural by going around here and there and adjusting the velocities so that occasionally one element or another stands out.

In Figure 3.23, you can see the velocity curve illustrated below the piano roll view of a drum track. Notice that every hit has its own particular value and that the strongest hits tend to be on the strongest parts of the measure.

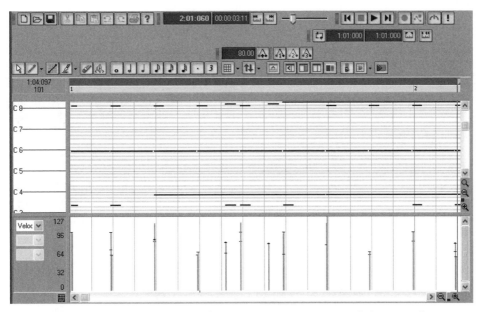

Figure 3.23 A natural-sounding velocity curve in a sequenced drum track.

Creating a Groove

Another feature that contributes a sense of natural realism to a drum track is the groove. A groove represents the characteristic way in which a drummer instinctively brings some sounds in slightly earlier or slightly later than expected, depending upon the feel that he or she wants to achieve. In this respect, swing also counts as being a natural part of the groove.

A common sound to apply a groove to is the snare. If the snare comes in consistently but slightly early, it gives a tight feel to the drumming, whereas if it comes in slightly later, this gives the opposite sense—a more relaxed and laidback feel. The amount of time by which a sound is brought in early or taken late is virtually negligible—literally milliseconds—yet it is surprising how much it can affect the feel of the drum pattern.

It is well worth spending time experimenting with grooves. Apart, perhaps, from the kick on the first beat, virtually any drum hit can be brought backward or forward slightly to create the kind of groove you want. A drummer, after all, is not a robot. Consequently, every hit is going to have that human element of response to the beat, which means that while some strikes will be dead on the beat, others will occur slightly before and after it. The best way to experiment is to turn the snap to grid function off and use your mouse to bring the notes forward or backward by varying increments. These increments are very small and often amount to only a small fraction of a thirty-second.

Many drum machines and sequencers have a groove function, which means you can select however many bars of your drums you want and apply that particular groove to them. Once you have applied the groove, you can use the mouse to adjust any of the hits individually where you think they can be improved. Grooves are used in all styles of music, and they are one of the ways in which a particular style and a more natural feel is brought to the drums.

Grooves are very popular in dance music, especially house, trance, and techno. The groove in this case does not just contribute to the feel of the drumming, but it also affects the way individual drum sounds tend to stand out from the often dense drum textures. In Figure 3.24, you can see a groove being applied to a house drum pattern.

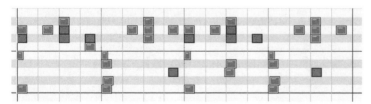

Figure 3.24 Groove applied to house drums (Track 10 on the audio CD).

The bottom layer is the kick drum, which is dead on the beat. Above that is the clap, falling on Beats 2 and 4. This has been placed slightly after the beat to give a nice, laidback sense. Above that is a tom-tom, the three hits of which have been freely placed where they feel right for the groove. All of the layers above that are auxiliary percussion instruments that create the ride element, and aside from the factor of swing, they are all fairly spot on the beat.

Many programs offer pre-programmed grooves, which are very useful as a starting point. To apply a particular groove, it is often just a matter of selecting the drum part and choosing the groove from a drop-down menu. If you have access to these, I would advise you to study the grooves available and try to see how the groove affects the feel of the drums. Once you get the hang of this, you will be in a position to develop your own grooves.

Using Fills

Another important feature of natural-sounding drumming is the fill. A fill is a flourish—often on toms, but also sometimes using the snare—that announces the end of one four- or eight-bar phrase of music and serves to introduce the next phrase. The first beat of the next phrase is then often punctuated through the use of a crash symbol. The fill is one of the areas where a drummer shows off his technical skill, which means that fills are often quite complex, involving a flurry of hits virtually in free time. They are also a test of the drummer's timing and ability to finish the fill dead on the first beat of the next bar.

Fills are notoriously difficult to write due to their complexity, the flexibility of timing involved, and the range of dynamics required to make a fill sound realistic. We will consider how to write two kinds of basic fill: a fill using toms and a fill that uses the snare and kick as the main components.

In Figure 3.25, you can see a typical tom fill. The feature that makes it typical is the way in which the fill starts off with the highest tom—Tom 1—and then works its way down through the other toms—2, 3, 4, and 5—to culminate in a final crash announcing the start of the next section of the music. Observe from this a number of important features. Playing the toms in this way gives a gradual descent in pitch, a descending scale of pitch

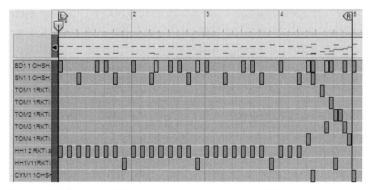

Figure 3.25 Tom fill (Track 11 on the audio CD).

values that starts with the smallest tom and culminates with the largest. This gives rise to an effect that is rather like accelerating or tumbling down a hill—its energy is cumulative and peaks with the sound of the crash at the beginning of the next bar. Notice as well that the ride has stopped playing, because it is impossible for a drummer to maintain this while playing the fill. And the snare is only struck when the player has a hand free with which to strike it.

In this next example—Figure 3.26—the snare and kick are used to provide the fill. Notice again that the fill is characterized by a flurry of accelerating activity, this time occurring on the kick and snare. And the crash is again used to increase the dramatic effect of the fill.

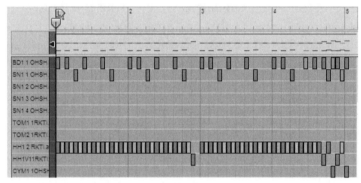

Figure 3.26 Kick and snare fill (Track 12 on the audio CD).

In an eight-bar drum pattern, you would tend to get a fill in the later part of the eighth bar and sometimes also a semi-fill at the end of the fourth bar. Fills need to sound spontaneous, so do not repeat fills in exactly the same way each time. Modify them in some way so that they sound like a live drummer spontaneously responding to the music.

Through use of fills to announce the ending of particular sections of the drum track, the drum track interfaces with and has a direct connection and bearing upon the structure of the music. This connection in turn will determine the points where it becomes suitable to introduce changes to your patterns in order to reflect changes in that structure— for example, a change from verse to chorus or vice versa.

Providing Color and Atmosphere

The ride is a functional element that gives the drum track a sense of continuity and motion. As a functional element, feasibly any drums or drum samples can be used to fulfill that function, provided that they sound right to the ear. Consequently, as long as the ride contributes that sense of continuity and forward motion, virtually anything that sounds right to you will do. For this reason, the ride offers a great degree of freedom for creativity, atmosphere, and color.

The main alternative to the use of hi-hats on the ride is the ride cymbal, used either instead of or as part of a pattern that mixes the sounds of both. This is particularly common in jazz drumming. Another way to add color and variety to the ride is through the use of tambourines and shakers. And because these would normally be played by a separate percussionist or percussionists, they can be treated very freely.

Another colorful element that can be introduced is the cowbell, and it is possible to create some great patterns that mix hi-hat and cowbells within the ride element. This offers another dimension of interest to the ride. Although providing that regular tap-tap, which gives the drums their sense of continuity, the rhythm created through the inter-action of the hi-hat and cowbell also offers another feature of interest for the ear. Other types of traditional drum samples you can use to add atmosphere and color are wood-blocks, claves, castanets, and clay or china drums.

All of these represent traditional ways of giving the drum track color and atmosphere. Within the context of electronic music, there is a wealth of sounds you can use to add style, color, variety, and atmosphere. There are reversed drum samples—such as reverse kicks, snares, cymbals, and hi-hats—samples of vinyl scratches and bursts of white or pink noise, electronic zaps, vocal hits, and exotic percussion instruments, such as the guiro, samba whistle, cuica, and cabasa. In fact there is no limit to the variety of such sounds you can use. Any sampled sound can be brought in and used in a percussive context. I once heard a drum track in which someone had sampled a person sweeping a broom over a sheet of cardboard. It sounded absolutely great.

Probably the best time to think about this type of drum sound is when you have laid down your three main functional elements and you feel that these work well together as a rhythm. Once you've accomplished this, you can explore ways to add variety, interest, color, and individuality to your drum track. Such sounds can be used in addition to, or sometimes even as a substitute for, the main elements. A common example of this is the use of a rimshot instead of the conventional snare. A rimshot is the sound created when the drummer strikes the metallic edge of the drum rather than the skin. This gives a beautiful sharp metallic hit.

Many of the options for using such sounds will fall within the domain of the general style of music that you are creating. Vinyl scratches are common in hip-hop but would sound out of place in jazz. So the next thing to think about is the style of music that you are creating and how that style reflects back on your approach to the writing of a drum track.

Features of Style: The Drum Kit

So far I have shown that a drum pattern has three essential functional elements: kick, snare, and ride. Although all drum patterns tend to use these three functional elements, the way in which they are used can vary depending upon the style of the music you are producing. And the style of music, in turn, will be a primary determinant for which kind of drum kit you select for your project.

The necessity for different kinds of kits stems from the fact that each style has its own characteristic range of drum sounds. A boomy kick that would be great for, say, hip-hop would be quite useless in a house drum track. Similarly, a hardcore kick would sound ridiculous if used in the context of a pop music drum pattern.

Ascertaining the character, timbre, and quality of the drum samples you'll need will require detailed and careful listening to the music of your chosen genre. What kind of kick is characteristically used? And what is the quality of the snares? These are the types of questions it is useful to ask when listening to the music. Once you have a clear idea of these, the audition, selection, and shaping of a suitable drum sample becomes much easier because you know exactly what you are looking for.

Fortunately, the designers and manufacturers of the hardware and software devices we use to produce our music call upon a wide range of expertise when it comes to matters of drum programming. Because of this, to find a suitable kit with which to start your project is often a matter of just selecting it from a menu: Techno Kit 3, Hip-Hop Kit 4, Disco Kit, Trance Kit, Brush Kit 1, and so on. You can also create your own kits from samples that you have collected from various sources, a process which will be discussed in Chapter 15, "Sampling." Having done this, the rest is just a matter of modifying that kit to suit your requirements.

Coupled with learning about the three primary elements involved in the creation of a drum pattern, you also need to listen very carefully to the styles of music you are interested in to learn about the way the style approaches the three primary elements of the drum pattern. These can vary significantly. In jazz, for example, drum patterns are often led from the ride, which leads to a situation in which the kick and snare can often be placed at more subtle points in the bar (see Figure 3.27).

In this example, apart from marking out the first beat of the bar, the kick plays a subordinate role to the ride. And a rimshot is used as a substitute for the snare. The ride has two interacting elements; the first is provided by the ride cymbals, and the second is provided by the colorful percussion of the tambourine, maracas, shaker, and cowbell.

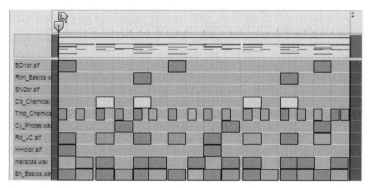

Figure 3.27 Basic jazz drum pattern (Track 13 on the audio CD).

Key Questions to Ask

When listening to the drums in the music of your chosen genre, you are looking for important features pertaining to the three elements. Here are some key questions you might like to ask:

- How is the kick used? Is it prominent or subordinate? What is the quality of the kick? Is it hard, soft, etc.? What kind of rhythmic patterns is the kick given? Are these simple or complex? Does the kick pattern have a forward rolling sense about it, or does it have a chopped quality?

- How is the snare used? Are substitutes for the snare used that often? What is the character of the snare sounds? Do they commonly have reverb?

- What is the ride like? Does it tend to use conventional hi-hats or ride cymbals? Is the ride element simple or complex? Does it have swing? Does the ride characteristically use other percussion instruments? Are certain types of samples commonly used (such as scratches, crackles, booms, vocal hits, and so on)?

Processing the Drum Track

Assuming that you have managed to create a decent working drum pattern, the next feature to consider is the processing of that pattern. By *processing*, I am referring to directing the output of the various channels of the drum machine/sequencer through various effects devices capable of modifying and affecting the drum sounds. Processing is a vital feature of drum programming because it can determine whether a drum track sounds lifeless and dead or vital and dynamic.

Through processing, the kick drum can be given more body and punch, the snare more power, and the hi-hats more presence. To achieve this, common insert effects used are compression, reverb, and delay. Compression is often applied, particularly to the kick to give it that punchy quality that enables it to stand out in the mix. Similarly, reverb is often applied to the snare, and the degree and type of reverb are determined by the type of snare sound you want. That huge-sounding rock snare you have heard was probably achieved through a combination of compression and reverb. A touch of reverb is often applied to the hi-hats as well, to give them more presence. Then there is delay, which is often used on auxiliary percussion elements, such as congas, claves, and so on, in order to produce a fuller, richer sound. Delay, you will soon discover, needs to be applied with great discretion.

Have a listen to Audio Track 14 on the CD. First you will hear the drums originally given in Figure 3.18 played without any processing. Immediately after, you will hear them as they sound once they have been processed: The snare was given a touch of delay and some reverb, and the hi-hats were given just a touch of reverb. Everything, including the kick, was then compressed.

Processing is very much a matter of experience coupled with a keen idea of what you actually want. It is possible to be very creative with processing and achieve some amazing effects through it. This applies especially to the whole drum track, which can be processed in numerous ways depending upon the exact sound you want. Filters, ring modulators, flanging devices—a great variety of effects can be applied with discretion to affect the final quality of the drums. Have you ever wondered how hip-hop drums get that lovely grimy quality? It is often because they are processed through an amp emulation effects unit. We'll talk more about the use of effects in Chapter 10, "Creative Use of FX."

Conclusion

Having considered various aspects of drum programming, let us now look back at what this chapter covered and put it together in such a way as to create a good general strategy for the intended creation of an effective and realistic drum track. First, I discussed the necessity of studying an actual drum kit in some detail. One of the main purposes of this is to enable you to mentally create a good working model of a drum kit, one that will help guide you toward making useful and productive choices as far as drum programming is concerned. Unless you know what a drum kit can do, the kind of sounds that it can produce, and how those sounds are produced, how can you expect to be able to write effectively for drums? The whole proposition is absurd. It would be like asking an engineer to design a bridge from an unknown material.

The next area of study was the importance of observing the playing techniques of live drummers. The logic of this is fairly easy to see: If you want to know about drumming, ask a drummer. We have all seen drummers at work all of our lives. Yet how close have we scrutinized what they are actually doing? Most people have never even given this area any thought, because normally we are in a mental position of being consumers. We are listening to and enjoying the sound, which is quite different from the frame of mind needed to learn more about drumming. To gain knowledge about drumming, you must adopt a new stance, one which involves actively observing and scrutinizing the process of drumming in great detail.

Studying a drum kit and observing drummers playing offer vital knowledge that can be brought directly to bear on the options and choices available to you for writing drums within your own particular studio setup. Whether you are using hardware/software drum machines or synthesizers/samplers that offer drum kit patches, you now know exactly what you are looking for when it comes to writing a drum track. A sampled drum kit containing maybe 120 different sampled sounds now presents you with no problems. You have developed a clear sense of priorities and orientation toward the necessary elements for your drum writing, and you know how to distinguish these from auxiliary or secondary elements. Your choices, in other words, are now informed choices based on your knowledge of drums and how they are played.

When it comes to composing an actual drum track, the first key ingredient is the composition of a decent working kick-snare pattern, and it is this pattern that lays down the basic working rhythm of the drum track. I highlighted the importance given to the backbeat as a response to the downbeat of the kick, and I provided numerous examples of simple yet effective kick-snare patterns to start you off on your own study, exploration, and production of such patterns. We looked at the principles of sequencing and extending such patterns, together with the role of secondary hits as a means of producing variation, contrast, and balance within extended drum patterns.

The next key area we looked at was the ride element—the regular drum stroke that imparts a sense of continuity and motion to the drum track. We discussed the role of open and closed hi-hats as examples of drum samples that fulfill this function, together with the various alternative possibilities for the ride, such as the ride cymbal, tambourines, and so on.

Having studied the role of the ride, the issue of creating a drum track became much simpler because it was shown to be essentially a three-stage process involving the three functional elements of the kick, snare, and ride. This process, in turn, offers a good working model and guide toward the simple and effective production of drum tracks.

The areas studied after this included information about the key areas you need to look at in order to make drum tracks sound natural and realistic. With music production software, it is very easy to create a lifeless and mechanical drum track that sounds as if it is being produced on a machine. And, of course, it *is* being produced on a machine. Yet by paying attention to certain ingredients, the drum track can, to some extent, be humanized and given feeling, style, and expression.

One such area is swing, a natural tendency to slightly delay the sounding of the weaker beats. We considered the role of swing in imparting a sense of feeling and groove to the drum track, and we discussed the means of achieving various degrees of swing. Another important area is the velocity curve of the drum track. A live drummer cannot play like a machine and therefore cannot produce hi-hats that all have a uniform velocity of 100. We covered the role of velocity in the creation of natural and realistic-sounding drum tracks, together with the necessity of adjusting the velocities of individual drum sounds to make them sound less mechanical and more lifelike and realistic.

A third key feature we considered was the groove resulting from drum strokes being played slightly before and after the required beat. The groove is a natural human feature of drumming, and by applying and using different grooves, the basic human feel of the drum track can be both enhanced and modified. The fourth key feature was the fill— that flourish of activity the drummer uses to announce the end of one section and the beginning of another. We discussed different kinds of fills, together with the necessity of developing different fills or variations of the same fill in order to counteract that mechanical and lifeless quality of a computer-generated drum track.

The next issue we considered dealt with color, interest, atmosphere, and style, qualities that can be imparted to the drum track through the use of secondary percussion instruments and samples, such as tambourines, maracas, vocal hits, and other such samples. We discussed the use of these in relation to the ride element, together with the important possibility of using such sounds as substitutes within the three functional areas of kick, snare, and ride.

This naturally led the discussion to the issue of style as it applies to the process of writing a drum track, because style is a factor that will determine the type of drum kit that will be used, together with its expected range of typical auxiliary and secondary drum samples. We also discovered how style has an impact upon the way in which the three functional elements are approached, an observation which led to the necessity for keen questioning about the role of those three elements within a given style.

Having looked at these important areas pertaining to the process of writing drum tracks, you are now in a very clear position to start producing your own drum tracks with confidence, backed up by the knowledge of the most important basic principles. Yet the issue does not end there. Modern music, particularly electronic music, uses a wide roster of drum samples and sounds whose origins lie in other cultures than our own. A simple example of this is conga drums. No drum kit would be complete without at least a few conga samples.

The use of such samples generally falls into a wider domain of drumming practice signified by the word *percussion*. To improve your ability to write for drums, therefore, it is also necessary to undertake a keen study of how to write for such percussion instruments and successfully incorporate them into your own drum tracks. This will provide the topic for the next chapter of this book.

4 Writing for Percussion

In Chapter 3, we discussed the functional roles of the drums of an acoustic drum kit. And by functional roles, I mean the job they do as part of a drum track. The kick provides the foundation for the rhythm, while the snare contributes backbone and structure. The ride on the other hand, measures time and pace and is the guarantor of continuity and a sense of forward motion. Because the instruments that perform this job are so important in the process of producing a drum track, they can be regarded as having a primary nature. In other words, they are the drums with the highest status.

This knowledge gives you an essential orientation when composing drum tracks because you know that your first job is to address the needs of those primary instruments—to lay down a kick, a snare, and a decent, working ride. Once you have done this you are virtually there, because you have created a decent, workable drum track. And this is why any discussion of drum programming begins with the role of the primary instruments.

Secondary Instruments and Samples

Once you have grasped the concept of the primary instruments, it is time to look at the huge range of secondary instruments and samples—that is, drum samples that play an additional or auxiliary role in the process of writing drum tracks. Among these, the most important group by far is the percussion instruments. Of course, every drum is feasibly a percussion instrument, so this term needs to be qualified. By the term *percussion*, I mean any drum kit sample of a non-electronic origin that is not an essential part of a standard acoustic drum kit, for example, a conga.

There are literally thousands of samples that belong to this category, and the inclusion of at least some of these samples as a part of various MIDI drum kits explains why those kits are so large. In addition to the conventional drum sounds, they also include a whole roster of percussion sounds. In this chapter, we will take a look at the role of percussion in general and discuss the key issues that surround the process of writing percussion parts as a part of your rhythm tracks.

There are two basic kinds of percussion samples you will use. The first is coloristic percussion. This category includes samples of tambourine, maracas, castanet, agogo bell, claves, woodblocks, triangle, finger cymbals, cowbell, cabasa, gong, bells, caxixi, shaker, guiro, piatti, cuica, and so on. The principle value of this kind of sample is one of color, in that its inclusion as part of a drum track lends both coloristic appeal and atmosphere. And when used appropriately, these samples can also be used to infuse your drum tracks with particular national and local atmospheres. A classic example of this is the samba whistle, the use of which offers an immediate suggestion of a South American carnival atmosphere.

Coloristic percussion can generally be used in two ways. First, it can be used as an addition to your normal kick-snare-ride pattern. In effect, this means that when you compose your drum track, you add additional color to it through the use of coloristic percussion samples. Examples of this type of use are the traditional finger snap used as an accompaniment to a drum track, or the use of castanets or tambourine to add a sense of style and exotic appeal to the drums.

Because the use of these would normally require another player or players, you are not constrained or limited by the drummer's two hands. Consequently, it is possible to create coloristic percussion parts of delicate intricacy. In see Figure 4.1, you can see an example of a ride part involving the use of some seven layers of colorful percussion instruments. (The tambourine enters at Bar 5, not shown here.)

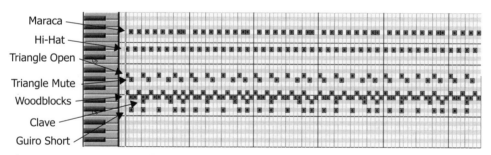

Figure 4.1 Percussion ride element (Track 15 on the audio CD).

Alternatively, you can use coloristic percussion as a substitute for one or more of the functional elements normally performed by the kick, snare, and ride. Examples of this are the substitution of, say, a sleigh bell sample for an open hi-hat or a woodblock hit for the conventional snare drum sound. And sometimes you will see a drummer deliberately add a coloristic percussion instrument to his kit. The most common example is a cowbell, generally used as an alternative ride instrument. Whichever way you care to use it, coloristic percussion offers many opportunities to spice up your drum tracks and give them both atmosphere and color.

The next type of percussion sample is the functional percussion sample. These are drum samples taken from drums that are not a general part of the conventional drum kit. A standard General MIDI kit contains numerous categories of functional percussion: taiko, djembe, baya, tabla, bongo, and conga. The exotic names given to these drums betray their origins, for they all form part and parcel of drumming systems and drumming traditions belonging to cultures other than our own. This is why they are called *functional* percussion—because in the countries of their origin, they all fulfill a primary and important role in the process of drumming.

These drums and the drumming traditions to which they belong have provided a perennial source of fascination for Western musicians. I am sure you have seen and heard the impressive spectacle of taiko drumming, a Japanese drumming tradition that goes back hundreds of years. To see and hear this is literally awesome, and for anyone interested in writing for drums, this particular type of drumming represents a fascinating topic. Yet it is but one tradition of many.

From our standpoint as music producers, we do not have the time to learn all of these traditions, especially in light of the fact that in the countries of their origin, these traditions often require many years of study to master. The music producer's primary interest is the way in which those traditions can be and have been used to enrich our own musical language and increase its spectrum of resources. But even then, to make effective use of these resources, it is important to find out what these drums are, how they are played, and the kind of sounds offered by them. This chapter provides a brief summary of some of the main types of these drums, together with some examples of patterns written using them.

Congas and Bongos

Along with bongos, congas are probably the best-known drums of ethnic origins to Western musicians, and we know about them primarily through their use in Latin American music. As a type of hand drum played with the hands instead of sticks, their characteristic sound has long enriched the colorful language of jazz. Indeed, a jazz band would not be complete without a percussion section that includes both conga and bongo. In other contexts, they provide a spectrum of percussion sounds that enriches many other musical styles—especially dance music, where their use has become a norm in many styles.

Congas often come in sets of three: a high-, medium-, and low-pitched drum. The timbre of each drum subtly changes depending upon how hard it is hit. Therefore, ideally you will need hard, medium, and soft samples of each of the three drums. You will also need samples of the different characteristic types of conga hits.

The primary hit is where the drum is hit cleanly in the center, which gives a nice, resonant tone. A slap is where the conga is hit nearer the edge, and this produces a shorter, crisper sound. Mute is where the head is immediately touched after the hit to stop the tone. A double hit is where two congas are hit at the same time. A finger roll is, as the name suggests, a rapid trill with the fingers, whereas a slide refers to a movement of the palm across the drum head. Finally, there are ghost notes, where the drum is hit very, very gently. These latter sounds can be obtained fairly easily by lowering the velocity of the hit and altering the sample start time in order to take off most of the attack. In this way, all you will hear is a really gentle drum tone.

In Figure 4.2 you can see an example of a conga pattern written using a software sampler. The drums used, together with the type of hit, have been labelled clearly.

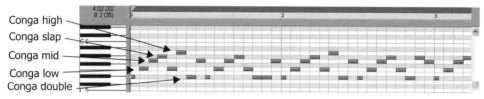

Figure 4.2   Conga pattern (Track 16 on the audio CD).

Bongos originate from a similar part of the world as congas, and although they are often used together and associated with each other, bongos have a very different kind of sound. They are normally played in pairs, one high-pitched and one low-pitched. The main strokes commonly found in sample banks are open (which is a hit near the center of the drum), a slap around the edge of the drum, a strike with a stick, and the typical flam and roll often found in bongo patterns. The latter are two of the techniques used to create the intricate drum patterns you often find with bongos, the flam being a quick double strike of the skin with the fingers, and the roll being a rapid trill with the fingers.

Daraboukas

The darabouka, also known as a dumbek or Arabic tabla, is one of the main drums used by percussionists in the Middle East (see Figure 4.3). Originally made from clay, they are normally played with the hands, with the drum resting on the lap. They are most commonly seen in the West through their role as accompaniments to belly dancing. The distinctive name *dumbek* given to this drum relates to the two main sounds that come from this drum—a *dum* followed by a *tek* (this syllable describing how the drum sound is vocalized rather than written). *Dum* is the deeper and softer sound obtained by striking the center of the head with the hand. *Tek* is the higher-pitched and much harder sound obtained when the edge of the drum is struck. There is also a third characteristic sound,

Figure 4.3 A darabouka.

ka, which is an equivalent sound to *tek* but is struck with the other hand. Intricacy in the drum pattern is obtained through delicate finger work, slaps, flams, and rolls, which are used to ornament the basic rhythm defined by *dum* and *tek*.

When learning the various rhythms of Middle Eastern music, the player first learns to vocalize the basic pattern using these syllables. There are many such patterns, and some of them have very unusual time signatures, such as 5/8, 13/8, 17/8, and so on. In Audio Track 17 on the CD, you can hear one of the most famous dumbek patterns, called *Ayyub*, which goes like what you see in Figure 4.4.

Having heard this, you will probably recognize it as also being one of the main underlying rhythms used in house music. It has a beautiful rolling quality, which makes it particularly good to dance to.

	1				2				3				4			
Dum	x				x			x				x				
Tek			x			x					x			x		

Figure 4.4 Middle Eastern dumbek pattern—Ayyub (Track 17 on the audio CD).

Tablas

Tablas are drums characteristically used in the rich traditions of Hindustani (North) and Carnatic (South) Indian music. They are a pair of drums with goatskin heads, with each drum tuned to produce a note of a particular pitch—normally note C for the larger drum, called *baya*, and note E for the smaller drum, called *tabla*. To play the tabla, the performer sits cross-legged on the floor and plays them with his fingers. The most important strokes are open and mute. Additionally, a pitch bend is often obtained on the baya by pressing the drum head with the palm.

The rhythmic patterns used in Indian music are called *tala*, and like the patterns of Middle Eastern music, they have a rich diversity and often involve what for us are unusual time signatures, such as 7/4, 11/8, and so on. The characteristic sound of the tabla is often used to provide color and enrichment to dance music drums, especially in styles such as psy-trance and house music. Figure 4.5 shows an example of a tabla pattern written using the Orkester Sound Bank Tabla samples in Reason 4.0.

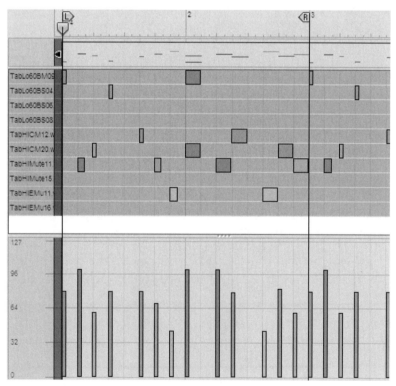

Figure 4.5   Tabla pattern (Track 18 on the audio CD).

Djembe and Udu

The djembe is one of the best-known and popular African drums, particular with those in the West who are interested in learning a drumming tradition. Made of wood with a skin head, it is played with the bare hands (see Figure 4.6). Aside from hard, medium, and soft samples, the most important strokes to get samples of are the open, mute, and slap. The open is a strike in the center of the head that produces the resonant low tone; the mute and the slap result from a strike near the rim of the drum. You can see and hear all three of these in the simple djembe pattern shown in Figure 4.7 and found on Track 19 of the audio CD.

Figure 4.6   A djembe.

	1				5				9				13			
Djembe Open	X								X							
Djembe Slap				X			X					X			X	
Djembe Mute			X			X		X			X			X		

Figure 4.7   Djembe pattern (Track 19 on the audio CD).

The slap is used to provide the backbeat, while the mute strike provides an effective ride element.

The udu is another famous African drum, originating from Nigeria (see Figure 4.8). It has a distinctly contrasting sound to the djembe on account of the materials of its construction. Starting out as a clay water jug, another hole was later added to improve its qualities as an instrument of percussion. The open bass tone of the udu has a beautiful resonance and is produced when the palm strikes this hole. You can see and hear this characteristic sound in the udu pattern shown in Figure 4.9 and found on Track 20 of the audio CD.

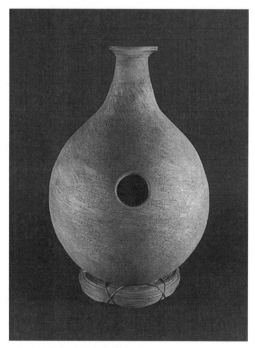

Figure 4.8   An udu.

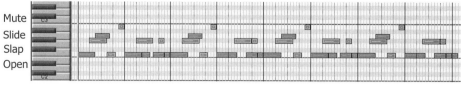

Figure 4.9   Udu pattern (Track 20 on the audio CD).

Writing Percussion Parts

Similar to writing for a conventional drum kit, it is well worth spending some time getting to know how particular functional percussion instruments are played. If you know how they are played, the various samples of percussion sounds available in your sample banks will start to make immediate sense to you. You will know, for example, that *conga high slap* means a sharp strike on the rim of the smallest drum of the set.

This way, you will gradually develop the ability to translate percussion samples into the actions required of a player to produce them. This, in turn, will help you be able to combine these samples to make an effective percussion track—that is, one that not only has rhythmic interest, but also has some kind of realism to it. It is a track that the listener feels is actually being played by somebody.

When writing for functional percussion, you can use two general approaches. The first is to use functional percussion as a substitute for a conventional drum track. An example of this is Ben Harper's song "Burn One Down," which replaces a conventional drum kit with djembe. The result is a really fresh and innovative-sounding approach to the rhythm track of the music.

The second approach is to use a functional percussion instrument alongside a conventional drum kit. In the case of dance music, which does not use a conventional drum kit anyway, this means using functional percussion in addition to the usual kick, clap, and hi-hat pattern.

Writing Functional Percussion as a Substitute

The most important point to realize when you are writing functional percussion parts is that the basic principles are the same as when you are writing for a conventional drum kit. If you studied Chapter 3 closely, you already know what those principles are. In effect, this means you are already well along the way toward writing effective functional percussion tracks. The knack is in knowing how to translate those principles into terms applicable to a different set of drums.

You can see a very simple example of this in the case of the dumbek. The relationship between the *dum* and the *tek* is the same type of polar relationship that you find between the kick and the snare, with the more resonant *dum* being parallel to the kick and the sharper and shorter *tek* being parallel to the snare.

To write an effective dumbek pattern, therefore, first you need to get a decent *dum-tek* main pattern. After you have done this, you need to provide the parallel for the ride element of conventional drum patterns. This is achieved by using the secondary softer strikes of the drum. That's all there is to it.

In terms of writing for congas and bongos, the same principle applies—the deeper open tones perform a kick-like function, while the sharper slaps perform a snare-like function. And again, the softer minor strikes are used to provide a ride element.

I want to demonstrate this by looking at a step-by-step approach to the writing of the conga pattern shown in Figure 4.2. First, you must lay down the equivalent of a kick-snare pattern over the space of one bar to give the backbone of the rhythm. This involves two samples—a double hit, which is the lower note in the diagram, and a slap, which is the upper note. See Figure 4.10.

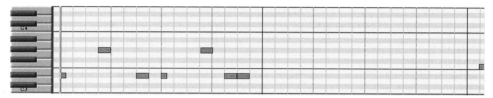

Figure 4.10   Double hit and slap conga pattern.

In this case, the double hit has been placed on semiquavers 1, 4, 7, 9, 14, and 15, and the slap on semiquavers 4 and 12. This gives a nice, clear pattern that provides an audible backbone rhythm. The next stage is to provide the equivalent of a ride element—that is, softer, less prominent drum hits that impart the important sense of motion to the rhythm. See Figure 4.11.

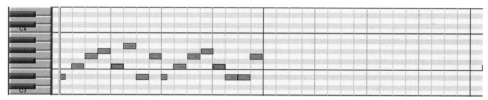

Figure 4.11   One-bar conga pattern.

In this example, these have been added on all of the otherwise empty semiquavers in order to create a sense of rolling motion. At this stage it becomes necessary to adjust the velocities of each individual hit, especially to make sure that the hits just added do not interfere with or dominate the backbone rhythm laid down in the first step. Having adjusted the velocities, you then need to apply an appropriate groove to the pattern. This can be done either by giving it a preset groove or, preferably, by creating your own groove.

Begin with the slaps, which are the focal points of the rhythm, bringing them slightly forward and/or backward depending upon the feel you want to create. And then go on to the secondary hits. The aim here is to impart a sense of naturalness to the pattern, as if it were being played by a live performer.

Having done this, the next stage is to copy and paste the pattern to Bar 2. After you have done so, make some minor alterations in the second bar to give the pattern some variation and interest. See Figure 4.12.

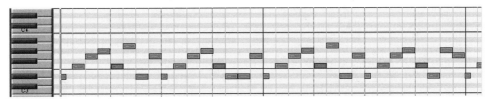

Figure 4.12 Two-bar conga pattern.

And there you have it—a nice and simple effective conga pattern. The final stage is to process the pattern—that is, to apply the necessary insert effects to it. For a basic conga pattern, the most important effects to apply are reverb and delay. Conga patterns are often processed with quite a bit of reverb because this tends to bring out the fullness of the open tones. Another trick commonly used is to apply a small amount of delay. Without being obviously audible, the slight echo of each drum hit caused by the delay tends to give functional percussion patterns a nice feeling of depth and resonance. If you have the ability on your sampler or drum machine, you can apply panning to good effect, too. Although your main elements would tend to be panned to the center, other related pairs of drum sounds can often be panned a touch left and right to good effect.

Realize that you can apply exactly the same principles to the creation of functional percussion parts using other types of drums. The most important feature is to decide what will be the key elements in terms of creating that kick-snare kind of relationship. In terms of tablas, for example, there is an obvious polarity between the lower tone of the gaya and the higher tone of the tabla. You can hear and study this polarity in Figure 4.5.

Writing for Functional Percussion as an Addition to Conventional Drums

The nice thing about functional percussion is that in a live situation, there would be separate performers there to play them. This gives you great freedom to develop quite complex and intricate percussion parts without worrying about what the drummer's two hands are capable of doing. Figure 4.13 offers an example in which a conventional drum part is supplemented by a complex tapestry of coloristic and functional percussion.

When you endeavor to write such parts, lay down the bass, snare, and ride first so that together they function as a complete self-contained drum pattern in their own right. Having done so, any other percussion you introduce will then function as a decoration

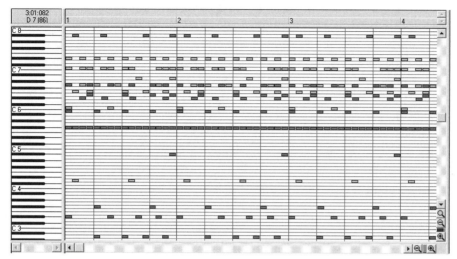

Figure 4.13   Matrix view of complex drum pattern (Track 21 on the audio CD).

and thickening of the ride element. This means you can add percussion elements layer by layer using your ear as the guide.

Do not be afraid to introduce these layers on very subtle levels, because even though they might not be directly audible, they all contribute to the overall color and quality of the drum track.

Another approach you might like to think about is writing in functional percussion elements as substitutes for conventional drum elements. This is a good ploy to adopt if you are looking for a fresh and more original-sounding drum track.

Conclusion

This chapter looked at the role of both coloristic and functional percussion instruments in the process of writing drum tracks. It showed that through the use of coloristic percussion, either as a substitute for primary drum elements or as a supplement to them, you can give conventional drum tracks much more interest, variety, atmosphere, and sparkle.

We looked at numerous types of well-known functional percussion instruments that we are liable to find in sample banks, together with the various kinds of sounds associated with their use. I gave examples of patterns that utilize these particular types of drums, as well as advice and support on how to write such patterns. Of course, you will have to find the approach that works best for you. The advice given here concerns the approach that best suits my way of working, which of course is only one way. Every person who writes his own music must find his own way and his own solutions to the problems that the process of writing music presents. Yet it can often be extremely helpful to see how somebody else solves those particular problems.

Drum programming is a huge topic, and many volumes could be written about it. This book can only hope to cover the main elements. That said, there is still a major element of drum programming that we have not yet covered, and that is the case of drum programming in dance music. This represents a different case than the process of writing a drum track for a conventional drum kit. Dance music does not tend to use such kits. On the contrary, it has developed its own unique spectrum of drum sounds and samples that are used in a very particular way. For this reason the next chapter of this book will concern itself with the issue of writing drum tracks for various styles of dance music.

5 Dance Music Drum Programming

Dance music drumming represents a separate branch of drum programming in its own right. This is because its beat is not referable in any way to the actions of a real drummer or the notion of a traditional drum kit. From the earliest days of dance music, when the styles of techno and house were still underground sounds, drums were often programmed using what have since become classic drum machines, such as the Roland TR-808, the TR-909, and the more functional, percussion-oriented TR-727.

When writing a dance music drum track, therefore, you don't feel that need to persuade the listener that he is listening to a real drummer at work, which also means that there is no need to make the drum track sound realistic in a conventional sense. There are absolutely no such pretenses in the programming of drums for dance music. The primary purpose of the beat is to make people want to dance, and as long as it does so, the drums are fulfilling their most important function.

Does this mean that writers and producers of dance music need not study traditional principles of drumming? No, it does not. These traditional principles represent the major foundations upon which drumming is based. And insofar as those foundations reveal the three essential functional elements of drumming, they are directly relevant to the writers of dance music. This is especially the case with a style such as drum and bass, because despite its rapid tempo, the principles of writing a good drum and bass drum pattern are essentially the same as those described in Chapter 3.

Therefore, although the purposes and means of production of dance music drums are in many ways different, you will still find the same essential principles at work. And without knowledge of those principles, a writer of dance music will go through a lot of trial and error to try to get their drum tracks to sound right and have the right feel. Save yourself a lot of time and just learn the basic principles.

The most important feature to grasp is that dance music has evolved its own particular equivalents of the three functional elements of kick-snare and ride. Once you know this and you know what those equivalents are, you are in a good position to begin trying to program dance music drums.

The Kick Element

In many well-known styles of dance music, such as house, trance, and techno, it has become more or less universal to use a kick drum on all four beats of the measure. This four-to-the-floor kick is generally required to be the most prominent sound in the music, and great efforts are made to ensure that no other sound exceeds the level of the kick. This is why when you come into the proximity of somewhere dance music is being played, the first thing you hear is the telltale boom-boom-boom-boom of the kick. Figure 5.1 shows this basic kick pattern.

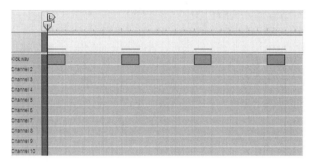

Figure 5.1   Dance music kick pattern.

Exceptions to the use of this pattern in dance music are commonly found in styles such as breakbeat, jungle, and drum and bass. In these cases, the three functional elements of the drum patterns used have a stronger connection with the traditional principles of drumming already discussed. The difference in this case is primarily in the electronic nature of the sounds used (such as the TR-808 kick drum so popular in drum and bass productions) and the predominant use of drum samples, such as the Amen Break. For writers of these styles, therefore, I refer you back to Chapter 3.

These exceptions aside, apart from differences in the type and quality of the kick, together with the characteristic use of different tempos, this four-beat kick pattern tends to be used across the board. Variants of this pattern are obtained through the insertion of secondary hits—that is, hits of the kick that have a lesser velocity. These can be placed anywhere between the four main beats, and depending upon how many of them there are, they determine whether the variant is a fairly simple or a complex one. The most common place for such variants is at the end of four- and eight-bar phrases.

When it comes to the selection and use of a kick drum, style is a strong determining feature. To write a dance music drum track effectively in a certain style, you need to answer beforehand certain essential questions with regard to the kick.

- What is the exact quality of the kick used in that style?

- Is it hard, soft, gentle, pounding, booming?

- How can I achieve that precise quality within my own setup?

- Where can I obtain suitable kick samples?

Because the kick is the most important sound you will use in a dance music track, it is essential to get that sound exactly right, no matter how long it takes. It is difficult to think of Detroit techno, for example, without its famous kick taken from the Roland TR-909 drum machine. Therefore, aside from very careful listening to the music of your chosen style, you also need to obtain suitable samples of kicks that do the job you are looking for. The Internet is a good place to start your search for suitable kick samples. Forums and groups devoted to particular styles of music can also provide a really useful source of information. Suffice it to say, spend as much time as you have to trying to get that perfect kick sound for the style in which you are writing.

The Snare Element

By *snare element*, I am not talking about the specific sound of the snare drum, but of the function normally performed by the snare drum as the provider of the backbeat. In dance music the backbeat is just as important as it is with many other styles of drums, the difference being that within a dance context it is normally (but not always) supplied by a clap.

As the provider of the backbeat, this clap would normally double the kick on Beats 2 and 4, as shown in Figure 5.2.

Figure 5.2   Backbeat clap in dance music.

Because of its relatively bright, sharp sound, a snare drum can be used effectively as a backup for the clap, but the snare needs to be adjusted to a level so that it provides only body and emphasis to the backbeat. As such, for the ear, the two sounds merge to become one.

The clap itself can also be positioned slightly before or after the kick, depending upon the type of groove you want to create. Putting it slightly forward for tight and slightly back for loose is a general guide. By adjusting it in this way, the sound of the clap is liable to be more prominent because its attack point is slightly different than the attack point of the kick.

You need to ask similar questions of the clap as you asked of the kick drum relative to the style of dance music you are writing. A sharp clap with plenty of reverb that would sound effective in hard dance would not be effective or appropriate in deep house. So again, my advice is to listen carefully to the music of your chosen style and be diligent in your search for and collection of appropriate clap samples for use in your tracks. Also, watch out for particular ways of processing the clap sound. A clap treated with delay proves very effective in some styles of techno.

The clap is a good sound to experiment with because it fulfills a function in providing a backbeat. As long as that function is adequately fulfilled, there is room for experimentation and variance with the sound used for this. So don't be afraid to try unusual sounds as a substitute for the usual clap. These could be electronic samples, rimshots, glitches, conga slaps, or some other suitably prominent sound.

The Ride Element

Dance music commonly uses a ride on both eighths and sixteenths. The choice of what to use depends upon the sense of pace required. A ride on the sixteenths gives a greater sense of pace than a ride on the eighths. In common with conventional drum tracks, the ride element is normally played by hi-hats, and it is common for all of the off-beat eighths to be on open hi-hats.

This ride element, coupled with the kick and the clap, gives rise to the basic template that represents the very core of dance music drum programming (see Figure 5.3).

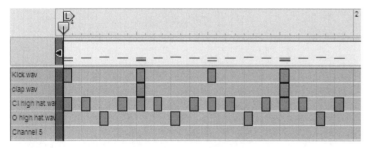

Figure 5.3 Template for dance music drum programming.

A strong feature of this template is its extension and repetition within four-, eight-, sixteen-, and thirty-two-bar sections. These tend to comprise the basic time units from which the structure of dance music tracks as a whole are built up, which means that at the end of each four-, eight-, sixteen-, and thirty-two-bar cycle, there tends to occur characteristic changes in the drums, which are the dance music equivalent of the conventional drum fill. Because the type of change can depend very much upon the style, careful study and listening to the music of the style concerned will reveal any norms in this area.

The core pattern given in Figure 5.3 is subject to infinite variations and permutations, both within a given style and in terms of the overall spectrum of different styles. For the dance music producer, it represents a case of careful study of these variations as they apply to his or her own particular style. And it is up to the individual writer's own inventiveness and ingenuity to come up with new ones. A working knowledge of this template represents just the beginning of this process.

To illustrate this point, in the following sections we will discuss some examples of different approaches to this template as found in a selection of different styles.

Speedcore

Within the faster, harder styles of dance music, such as speedcore, the tempo alone obviates the use of any really fancy percussion. So often all that is required is a hard-pounding kick on the main beats of the measure, the harder the better. For people I know who write in these styles, their motto tends to be "harder, faster, darker," and this motto is applied to all areas of the music.

To obtain the right kind of dense quality to the kick, several kick samples are often combined. For example, you might merge the sound of one kick that has a really strong attack with another that has a strong middle. When combined, the two qualities merge to create that super-hard kick sound you want. The resulting sound is then typically overdriven, pumped up with reverb, and then compressed. Variety in the drum track is created through the use of double strokes, triplets, and various kinds of kick-stutter that interrupt the incessant pounding of the kick (see Figure 5.4).

Figure 5.4 Speedcore kick pattern (Track 22 on the audio CD).

Within this style of dance drum programming, contrast is achieved by creating passages that suddenly switch to drum patterns based on the half-beats as opposed to the quarters. This calls for a more conventional type of drum pattern that effectively operates at exactly half the speed of the track. Within the 170 to 180 BPM range, you can also introduce drum and bass breaks, which offer a nice contrast to the usual four-square kick pattern. You can easily create such patterns by using the basic principles of kick-snare-ride, as discussed in Chapter 3.

Hardcore

As the tempo relaxes toward dance styles such as hardcore (150 to 170 BPM), the use of additional drum elements becomes more feasible. Here you can begin to see the full use of the template described in Figure 5.3—that is, the common use of a clap as a substitute for the snare on Beats 2 and 4, and a ride element created through open hi-hats on the off-beat eighths. Closed hi-hats are also often used on the on-beat eighths in order to back up the kick and give the kick part more crispness and definition.

Reverb is not used on the kick so often in this type of style, although a touch of reverb can be put on the open hi-hats to give them more presence. Double hits on the kicks are common at the end of four- and eight-bar phrases, as are fills involving quarters moving up to eighths, to sixteenths, to thirty-seconds, and so on. Like the famous snare-drum roll of trance music on the thirty-seconds, these are often used prior to a breakdown, where more melodic material tends to receive the focus.

Figure 5.5 shows the three main functional elements. Over this core you can lay various other percussive sounds that fulfill the function of adding color, atmosphere, variety, and interest. These can include anything from conventional tambourines, shakers, and functional percussion instruments to vocal hits, glitches, electronic sounds, and any other kind of drum sample—taken straight or reversed—that fulfills the artistic purpose required.

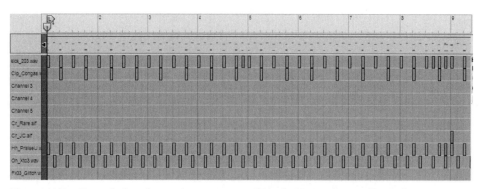

Figure 5.5 Generic hardcore drum pattern (Track 23 on the audio CD).

Hard Dance and Trance

Both hard dance and trance styles tend to follow to the letter the template shown in Figure 5.3. The difference between them with respect to drum programming often lies mostly in the quality of the kick drum. In the hard dance style, a very hard, resounding kick tends to be used, while in trance—especially the more melodic and uplifting variety—a softer and gentler approach to the kick may be found. And characteristic of the more general trance style are the use of reverse cymbals to announce structural changes, snare-drum rolls at the end of thirty-two bar sections, and kicks to which a huge hall reverb has been applied to be used as punctuating hits (kick-bombs).

You can hear an example of this type of hit rounding off Track 24 on the audio CD (see Figure 5.6).

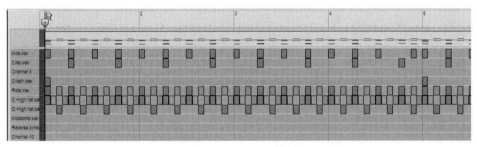

Figure 5.6   Basic trance drum pattern (Track 24 on the audio CD).

This type of pattern includes only the important functional elements. Color and variety are nearly always added through the use of other percussion.

Psychedelic Trance

The development of psy-trance was strongly influenced by early Goa trance of the late 1980s. Drum programming within this style is a matter of taking the template given in Figure 5.3 and infusing it with color and atmosphere through the use of characteristic psy-trance drum samples. One of the best known of these is the vibraslap.

Figure 5.7 uses two such samples. The pattern is presented as a grid (in which each column represents a sixteenth note) because the drums were sequenced on different channels, thereby making it awkward to present as a screenshot.

The kick is in the usual places, while there is a delayed and very subtle backbeat on the snare at 7 and 15. The ride is on conventional hi-hats. The other samples used are for style, atmosphere, and color: the two vibraslaps, the throbbing bass tones, and the jungle sounds sample.

	1				5				9				13			
Kick	X				X				X				X			
Conga														X		
Cl Hi-hat	X	X			X		X	X	X				X			X
O Hi-hat			X			X				X				X		
Vibraslap 1		X			X	X			X				X			X
Vibraslap 2			X							X						
Snare					X								X			
Bass Hit	X			X	X				X	X	X					
Jungle Sounds	X															

Figure 5.7 Psy-trance drum pattern (Track 25 on the audio CD).

Note: Any short, snappy drum sound can be turned into a vibraslap effect by sequencing it as four 64th notes, which together make up a sixteenth (see Figure 5.8).

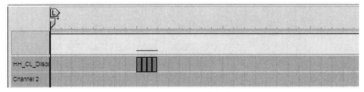

Figure 5.8 Sequencing a vibraslap effect.

Techno

Although techno uses the major elements of the template given in Figure 5.3, the major difference as far as techno is concerned is in the use of auxiliary percussion samples that veer strongly toward the electronic side—that is, bleeps, buzzes, and other such sounds that, speaking of the modern futuristic age of technology and robotics, prove such an inspiration for techno productions.

Techno is one of the oldest styles of dance music, and techno drums were originally written on drum machines. Even today, the producers of techno still retain a great fondness for the sounds of classic drum machines such as the Roland series: the TR-505, 606, 707, 808, and 909. Therefore, should you wish to produce techno, it would be well worth your while to hunt down samples from these old drum machines. Some of the kicks available have not yet been bettered for the purposes of techno.

Hardcore Techno

Techno has many variations of style, ranging from the harder and faster styles, such as hardcore techno, to the softer, gentler, and slower styles, such as minimal and Detroit techno. The relative hardness of the style is often reflected in the nature of the kick, which can range from being hard and pounding to quite gentle. Figure 5.9 shows an example of a pattern in the hardcore style. Observation of the grid shows that the template given in Figure 5.3 is more or less adhered to. The kick is on Beats 1 through 4, the clap is on Beats 2 and 4, while the ride is in eighths. The additional elements that give the drums their distinctive hard techno character are the distorted kick samples.

	1				5				9							16
Kick	X				X				X				X			
Clap					X								X			
Hi hat	X		X		X		X		X		X		X		X	
Snare roll sample							X								X	
Filtered snare	X			X			X		X				X			
Distorted kick 1			X				X				X				X	
Distorted kick 2	X			X			X		X		X		X			

Figure 5.9 Hardcore techno drum pattern (Track 26 on the audio CD).

Minimal and Detroit Techno

Both minimal and Detroit techno, as well as being typically slower in tempo, have a much more intimate sound to their drum tracks. And the drums of minimal techno are often characterized by their clarity and sparseness. Every drum sound employed within the track has to count. The drum sounds used are often samples from some of the old classic drum machines, and everything about the drum track is very carefully tuned and crafted. Figure 5.10 shows an example of a Detroit techno drum pattern.

Kick	X				X				X				X			
Ride	X		X		X		X				X				X	
O Hi-hat	X			X				X				X				
Cl Hi-hat		X	X	X		X	X	X		X	X	X		X	X	X
Conga			X								X					
Bongo					X								X			
Triangle	X	X	X	X	X	X	X	X	X	X	X	X	X	X	X	X
Vocal Hit													X			
Vinyl Crackle					X								X			

Figure 5.10 Detroit techno pattern (Track 27 on the audio CD).

The kick is in the usual points of the bar, as is the ride provided by the closed hi-hat. Open hi-hat is used to back up the kick, while there is an independent ride cymbal pattern superimposed over the continuous hi-hats. Instead of a clap, a bongo is used to provide the backbeat, and this has been shifted from its usual place on 5 and 13 to 7 and 15. The conga in turn provides a support to the bongo on 4 and 12. Color and atmosphere have been added using a muted triangle sample, a vocal hit processed with delay, and a vinyl crackle sample to provide a bit of dirt to the drum track.

Tribal Styles

The styles known as tribal represent an unusual and difficult case for drum programming, because in this case the drumming and percussion elements are the major elements of the style. Aside from the addition of vocal and other samples to add interest and atmosphere, the drums provide the main substance of the music. They literally *are* the music, and the drum track is often so dense as to leave little room for anything else. Writing drums in this style requires the careful layering of separate percussion elements over an embedded kick drum.

Each element is usually on its own channel and has its own characteristic pattern. And there is no real limit to the number of patterns that can be laid over one another. You are aiming to create a complex tapestry of drums, the emphasis of which is primarily on the gradual transformation of the colors and timbres that result from their combination and respective processing. The example in Figure 5.11 uses 16 channels; on each a separate software drum machine is operating and producing its own pattern as a contribution to the overall mix.

Figure 5.11 Tribal techno drumming (Track 28 on the audio CD).

Figure 5.11 gives some idea of the complexity of the different layers. To create this kind of drum patterning, lay down your kick initially and then create your separate layers one by one, making sure that they all work together. To do so, you will need large sample banks of drum sounds from every possible source you can find. Start collecting now and never stop. The more drum samples you have, the greater the freedom you will have with respect to writing drum tracks.

House

Like techno, the term *house* refers to a large cluster of styles ranging from the slower styles of ambient and deep house (110 to 125 BPM) to the harder and faster styles of Chicago, New York, and tech house (up to about 140 BPM). Like trance styles, the drum programming used in house tends to have a continuity of style, making it rather pointless to look at many styles individually. House drum patterns tend to begin with the template given in Figure 5.3—that is, a four-to-the-floor kick, a clap on Beats 2 and 4, and a ride on the hi-hats, with the open hi-hats tending to be on the off-beat eighths. House drum patterns are generally characterized by a strong swinging quality (see Figure 5.12).

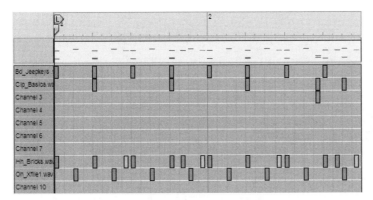

Figure 5.12 Basic house drum pattern (Track 29 on the audio CD).

If you can learn this template, you will have a good foundation from which to start applying the features that belong specifically to your chosen style, whether this be deep house, electro-house, minimal house, and so on. It all begins with this basic pattern, and stylistic differences in house drum patterns tend to be due either to the use of additional samples brought in to add color and atmosphere or to unique ways of processing the drum sound (such as the French house sound—associated with Daft Punk—with its characteristic use of filtering and side chaining). The house style also characteristically employs live sources of sounds, whether these are soulful vocals, sax solos, or live percussion players.

Typical variations of the template given in Figure 5.12 can include the use of secondary kicks or toms to create a strong underlying rhythm. You can see an example of this type of pattern in Figure 5.13.

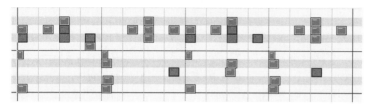

Figure 5.13   Classic house drum pattern (Track 10 on the audio CD).

The bottom layer is the kick, and above that is the clap. The next two layers up are the tom and the secondary kick, which with the main kick on Beats 1 through 4, gives the pattern its distinctive rhythm. The other elements are the ride on sixteenths, to which swing has been applied.

Another common variation is the use of functional percussion elements, such as congas, bongos, and so on. A good example is the deep house drum pattern in Figure 5.14, which uses a conga as a substitute for the conventional house clap.

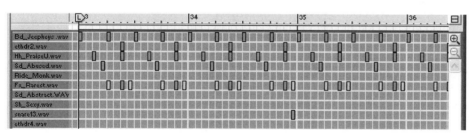

Figure 5.14   Deep house drum pattern (Track 30 on the audio CD).

In this pattern the conga is providing a delayed backbeat, while the ride is provided by the hi-hats on the off-beat eighths. And a gentle snare drum is used to anticipate and support the second and fourth beats of the kick in order to give it emphasis at these points.

Another very common technique is to use samples, vocal hits, and so on as conventional drum substitutes. In Figure 5.15, a Rhodes chord stab is being treated as a percussion element.

Kick	X			X			X			X			
Secondary Kick								X					
Clap				X						X			
Cl Hi-hat	X			X		X	X			X	X		X
O Hi-hat		X			X			X			X		
Chord Stab		X											
Bongo					X						X		
Claves										X	X		(Bar 4)
Vinyl Crackle		X			X			X			X		
Reverse Cymbal											X		(Bar 8)

Figure 5.15 House drums with chord stab (Track 31 on the audio CD).

The kick and secondary kick create the basic rhythm, while the clap provides the usual backbeat. The ride is on the closed and open hi-hats, while all of the other samples, including the Rhodes chord stab, are used to add color and style.

Processing Your Drum Track

The principles discussed in Chapter 3 work just as well for writing dance music drums. Primarily, you need to work on the three functional elements, which in Chapter 3 were described as kick, snare, and ride—with these terms referring to functions rather than sounds. Consequently, the sounds you use to fulfill those functions are a matter of your own artistic choice. In this respect, it does not matter whether you use a clap, a conga slap, an electronic hiss, or a vocal sample to fulfill the function of the snare element. Similarly, the ride can employ any number of elements, used either in addition to or as a substitute for the conventional hi-hats. The complexity of the ride is again up to you. You might want to create a dense ride consisting of dozens of separate elements. That is great as long as they all work together.

You will probably find it helpful to put each separate element that you create for your drum track on a separate channel. In this way you can process each element separately. This is very important with dance music, because some of the most important work you will do will be processing the sound—that is, applying insert effects to it. You will certainly want to compress your bass drum, for example. And you will also need to decide whether to alter the sound of your kick through the application of other effects.

Overdrive is a very common effect applied to a kick, and through use of overdrive you can even get your kick to sound like a bass tone—a common effect used in hardcore techno and gabba. Another effect that has been used on the kick is reverb. A kick treated with reverb has become one of the characteristic features of the comparatively new style of dance music called *hardstyle*. If nobody had ever bothered to experiment with applying different kinds of effect to a kick, this feature never would have been discovered. So feel free to be creative in this sphere.

Processing is a consideration that applies to every element of your drum track. Processing your hi-hats through a filter, a flanger, or a phaser produces great variations of sound within your hi-hat parts. Similarly, processing your congas with multi-tap delay can make a few simple drum hits sound like a conga wizard playing. So again, feel free to be totally creative in this sphere, and spend as much time as you can experimenting with applying different effects or effects chains to your drum sounds.

Processing is also a feature relevant to the entire drum track. Routing the drum track through a filter and then gradually adjusting the filter frequency and/or filter resonance is a trick that has been used for years. And through automation, you can affect your drums with an insert effect, such as a flanger, for a space of perhaps only one bar. This is a common effect in techno, and it can increase the interest and variety of your drum tracks enormously. For more information on this topic, see Chapter 10, "The Creative Use of FX."

Drums for Punctuation

There is another use of drums and instruments of percussion in dance music that has not yet been mentioned, and that is their use for the purpose of structural punctuation and the more general purpose of creating atmosphere within your work. Now, what do I mean by punctuation? Think of it this way: When you are writing words, there is a whole series of signs that do not belong to the functional alphabet, but that are used to indicate the way in which the writing is structured. These signs are the punctuation. Examples are the comma and the period. Through use of punctuation, the written word is able to both breathe and acquire a structural definition, which enables us to communicate through words more effectively.

You can say exactly the same of music. Percussion instruments are often used for the purposes of punctuation—that is, to indicate where sections of the music begin and end or where a major structural change is about to take place. A perfect example of a percussion instrument whose function is primarily for the purposes of punctuation is the crash cymbal. The crash is often used at the end of and during a fill in order to highlight the fact that a structural cycle in the development of the music is finished and a new one is about to begin. This is an excellent example of the use of percussion as a tool of punctuation.

Another example is the reverse cymbal sound. When the cymbal sound is reversed, the sound envelope acquires the opposite characteristics: It starts off really quiet and then gradually gets louder to culminate in the peak. You can see this in Figure 5.16, where at the top you can see a depiction of the ordinary cymbal sound and at the bottom you can see the same cymbal sound reversed.

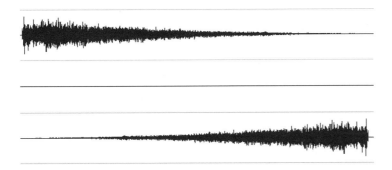

Figure 5.16 Comparison of the waveforms of cymbal and reverse cymbal sound.

This makes the reverse cymbal sound a very useful one for announcing the impending arrival of an important musical event. Although this effect might have been overused in trance music of the late '90s, it can still be used today, albeit in a more subtle, original, or thought-provoking fashion. If you are a Reason user, check out Doru Malia's Reverses refill, which offers lots of useful reverse cymbal sounds.

Another use of a drum sound that serves only the function of punctuation is the kick bomb popularized in Darude's track, "Sandstorm." The kick bomb is simply any kick drum sound to which a massive hall reverb has been applied. This type of effect can also be applied to any other drum sound, and at low levels of volume such sounds can be very atmospheric.

Conclusion

This chapter showed that the principles applicable to writing dance music drum tracks represent a natural extension of those principles discussed in Chapter 3. It is just a matter of knowing how and why those principles have been adapted for the purposes of dance music writing. We discussed the importance of the three elements of the kick, snare, and ride and gave individual treatment and observation to these elements individually.

This chapter presented a basic template for dance music drum programming, and I showed you that this template tends to run across the board of many dance music styles. The secret to writing a good dance music drum track lies in knowing how to adapt that template to the particular style concerned.

We looked at numerous examples of dance music drum tracks, and although it was not possible to consider every single dance music style, the principles of adaptability and of getting the sounds right for that particular style were shown to be major features underpinning the writing of an effective dance music drum track.

Having considered, over the space of three chapters, the basic features underlying the writing of drum tracks of various types and styles, we must now look at other vitally important elements involved in writing and producing your own music.

6 Common Values

Chapters 3, 4, and 5 spoke of the essential knowledge you need to write a drum track for your music. Generally the drum track is but one element of a piece of music, although you shouldn't forget that for some styles of music, the drum track is *the* most important feature. Tribal styles of dance music, influenced strongly by the traditions of African drumming, represent prime examples of this. These styles are modern electronic equivalents of the music of the drum, and within them, the drum remains the supreme element.

These styles are perhaps exceptions, as may be some styles of ambient music, where the rhythm track sometimes is virtually nonexistent. Focusing instead on creating slowly transforming organic beds of sound, ambient music can have a timeless quality that places it far beyond any sense of a beat. This is why ambient styles of music are good to listen to for relaxation: When we listen to them, our heartbeat tends to slow, and we gradually become more calm and relaxed.

If tribal and ambient musical styles represent opposite extremes with respect to the rhythm track, then between them lies most of the music with which we are familiar—music that has melodic leads, basses, harmonies, riffs, sound effects, and so on, all enhanced and supported by a rhythm track. Having considered the basic principles underlying the process of how to write a rhythm track, the next issue is to consider all of these other very important ingredients of a track.

To bring these elements into a clear compositional perspective, we need to realize that as computer musicians, many of our musical values have been unconsciously inherited from and shaped by earlier types of music. In this respect, the music of the Classical era probably represents the strongest and most potent influence on our musical values. Mostly consisting of a strong, lyrical melody supported by a clear bassline and guided by a simple chord progression, these values are still strongly sought after today in our world of computer-generated musical tracks (see Figure 6.1).

The writer and producer of computer music therefore needs to acquire certain basic skills above and beyond the ability to produce a decent drum track. These include

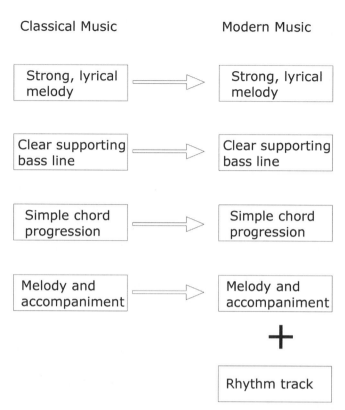

Figure 6.1 Continuity of values between classical and modern styles of music.

the ability to write a good melodic lead, a nice, clear supporting bassline, and a decent harmony or chord progression. Over the next series of chapters, we will look closely at these skills, and in particular the knowledge needed to acquire them.

Bass, Lead, and Harmony

Along with the rhythm track, the bass, lead, and harmony are extremely important features of any musical production. Representing the main melody, the lead can exist independently of the others. Hence you can hear a good song on the radio and then find yourself whistling the tune as you go about your daily business. This shows that the lead is generally the most important and recognizable feature of a piece of music for us.

Some music consists of just pure melody. An Irish jig played on a fiddle is a good example. This kind of music is called *monophonic*—that is, one-voiced. It is a type of music that goes far back into history, long before musicians ever learned to play in harmony with one another. Since the development of musical harmony, however, monophonic music tends to have had a more limited appeal for us, and we have all learned to appreciate and enjoy the much more complex and sophisticated sound that comes from musicians all playing together.

When it comes to the sound of ensemble playing, we have all learned to listen for and distinguish between two important elements: the lead and the bass. The importance of these two parts for a piece of music cannot be underestimated. The bass represents the lowermost melodic part of a piece of music. It therefore offers that all-important foundation upon which all of the upper parts, including the melodic lead, rest. The lead itself represents the main melody, which is often, although not always, the uppermost part. And even when it is not uppermost, the lead represents the important melodic part that gives the music its clear identity. It is the main melody, the tune by which the music will be remembered.

The issue of musical harmony is an important consideration here, for this arises automatically from the fact that as soon as you have lead and bass playing together, you also create the important element that is the relationship between them. This relationship is called their *harmony*. As representing the lowermost notes of a piece of music, the bassline has an obvious role as the supporter of that musical harmony. Automatically, this means that to be able to write an effective bassline, for example, you need a knowledge of or at least a strong feel for musical harmony. It is no good to write a bassline that has nothing to do with the lead. The bass needs to complement the lead and offer support for the harmonies above it.

For the bass to complement the lead, the first prerequisite is that both lead and bass are in the same key. I have seen many novice music composers and producers struggling in this area, and despite the fact that they have been very capable of producing effective basslines and beautiful melodic leads, they have not managed to get them working together very well. Primarily, this is because they have been writing their bass and leads in different and often clashing keys.

If your lead is in C major and your bassline is in E♭ minor, the two will clash, and between them they will produce a dissonant, jarring harmony. For many music producers, this is perhaps very obvious. Yet you would be surprised how often this simple problem occurs. To remedy this, you must undertake some important learning, and this includes learning all about different scale systems, keys, chords, and chord progressions. You can make a good start with this by studying the first book of this series, *Music Theory for Computer Musicians* (Course Technology PTR, 2008).

This book will impart to you all of the essential music and theoretical knowledge that you will need to be able to write professional-sounding music tracks—that is, tracks in which the bass and lead work together properly and where the harmony is guided by a clear and strong chord progression. For all music composers and producers, this is undoubtedly essential knowledge, and the sooner you can make a start with this the better.

Conclusion

In a sense this short chapter represents an interlude—that is, a brief pause that underlines the importance of acquiring certain basic knowledge before you proceed to studying the principles involved in writing basslines, melodic leads, and decent harmony fills. These principles will represent the topic of the next few chapters. Chapter 7, "Producing Basslines," will discuss the important issue of writing effective basslines. Chapter 8, "Writing Melodic Leads," will then go on to discuss the writing of melodic leads. Having considered both basses and leads, you can then, in Chapter 9, "Melody, Bass, and Harmony," look at the all-important relationship between bass and lead—a relationship where the issue of musical harmony becomes very salient.

7 Producing Basslines

The last chapter covered the relationship between the melodic lead and the bass-line, and how it is necessary for them to complement one another. We'll talk more about this subject in Chapter 9, "Melody, Bass, and Harmony." In this chapter, though, the primary concerns are the principles involved in writing a good, clear, and effective bass line.

You can learn much about the process of writing basslines by watching and listening to good bassists. Think of the bassist in a jazz combo, for instance. Here, a popular instrument to provide the bass is the double bass, whose strings are plucked with the fingers. The double bass is a huge instrument, and to change the pitch of the note, the bassist needs to slide his fingers up or down the long neck of the instrument to the necessary point where the string can be stopped. This in itself precludes any really fancy figuration or rapid note-work. Provided the bassist turns out the right notes to support the harmony of the music, his job is virtually done. The rest is style, flair, and skill on the part of the performer.

From this observation you can learn one of the first important principles of writing a bassline: Keep it simple. The sounds of a bass instrument are deep and heavy. And just like the foundations of a house, they need to be strong and firm to support the activity that goes on above them. For this reason, patterns of bass playing tend to be strongly anchored, rather than scurrying all over the place. The exception to this is perhaps the bass break, when the other performers step back to give the bassist a chance to show off his skills.

Although the double bass mentioned a moment ago is suitable for some styles of music, for most pop and rock bands the bass instrument of choice is the bass guitar, whose stronger tones are capable of carrying and supporting the sounds of all of the other instruments. A study of the bass instrument itself and the way in which bassists play it proves very instructive should you want to learn how to write good basslines.

Like the double bass, a bass guitar has four strings tuned by fourths to the notes E, A, D, and G (see Figure 7.1). Unless the bass is a fretless bass, frets are placed at every semitone rising upward toward the bridge. To play a particular note, the player presses the string firmly against the fret at the required point.

G string	G#	A	Bb	B	C	C#	D	D#	E	F	F#	G	G#	A	Bb	B
D string	D#	E	F	F#	G	G#	A	Bb	B	C	C#	D	D#	E	F	F#
A string	Bb	B	C	C#	D	D#	E	F	F#	G	G#	A	Bb	B	C	C#
E string	F	F#	G	G#	A	Bb	B	C	C#	D	D#	E	F	F#	G	G#

Figure 7.1 Bass guitar tuning.

The kind of sound produced depends upon how the string is plucked. There is the finger-bass sound produced when the string is plucked with the soft, fleshy pad at the front tip of the finger, which produces a nice, resonant bass tone. Then there is the pick-bass produced by plucking the string with a plectrum which produces a more crisp, metallic sound. Finally, there is the slap-bass sound produced when the player plucks the string in such a way as to cause the string to slap back on the fingerboard. This produces a much more rhythmically articulated and percussive sound.

Providing a Bassline

When providing a bassline for a song, the first thing a bassist needs to know, or pick up, is what the chords of the song are—in other words, the chord progression. If the bassist knows this, together with the precise timing of the chord changes, then he is in a position to be able to provide an effective working bassline. This is because the chords themselves will determine the best notes for the bassist to play. Say, for example, that at a particular point in a song, a chord of A minor occurs. A chord of A minor has three notes, which are A, C, and E. So the bassist knows in advance that whatever kind of bass pattern or riff he is playing, he needs at this point to play it around the notes A, C, and E.

Figure 7.2 depicts the four strings of the bass (which are tuned by fourths as E, A, D, and G, working from the bottom up) together with the various frets. The circles show the finger positions necessary to be able to play the notes of the chord of A minor. Note A is produced by the A open string (signified by a white circle), Note C the third fret of

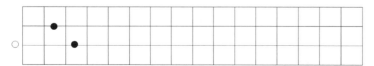

Figure 7.2 Fret positions for the notes of the chord A minor.

the A string, and Note E the second fret of the D string. Or at least this is one way of playing the notes concerned.

In fulfilling the requirement of providing the bass notes for this particular chord, certain characteristic features, styles, and options are available to the player. These in turn reflect back upon the fundamental principles involved in writing a bassline. And please note that although you, as a computer musician, might not be writing your bass parts for a bassist to actually play, the principles of writing a good bassline have a strong history and tradition established through the practice of bass playing. By learning those principles, you will consequently learn how to both write an effective bassline and adapt those principles for your own purposes.

Root Basses

One such option is for the bassist to play just the root of the chord, which in this case is Note A. This is by far one of the most common options for a bassist when providing a bassline. The Beatles' "A Hard Day's Night" provides a prime example of this type of bass playing. In the case of our model chord of A minor, all that root note playing would require is the plucking of the A open string. This option, involving but one note, is clearly the simplest to achieve.

However, in a real situation, the bassist would not pluck the A string at random. He would be keenly listening to the other parts, especially the rhythm track, and he would try to play something that complemented and enhanced it. This is a very important observation because it shows that the bassist, as well as providing the necessary notes to support the harmony and lead, also has an important role in supporting the rhythm track. And these are two of the major considerations behind writing a good bassline: There are the notes played by the bassist, and there is the rhythm with which they are played. And it is this rhythm that, when played in a repeating driving sense, creates what is called a *bass riff*.

Coming back to the root Note A mentioned a moment ago, let us consider some simple options. The note can be repeated at regular intervals. Repetition on the quarters is one such option (see Figure 7.3).

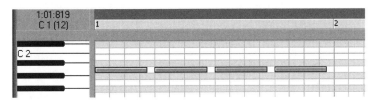

Figure 7.3 Note repetition on the quarters.

A more interesting option is to play bass on the eighths. This has more pace and serves to back up the ride element of the drum track (see Figure 7.4).

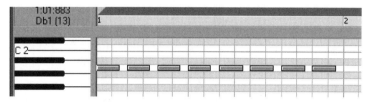

Figure 7.4   Note repetition on the eighths.

Finally, there is note repetition on the sixteenths. This kind of bass pattern has a lot of energy and pace (see Figure 7.5).

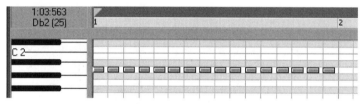

Figure 7.5   Note repetition on the sixteenths.

You can hear all three of these following one another in quick succession, moving from quarters to eighths and then to sixteenths, on Track 32 of the audio CD.

Another option for playing bass on a single note is to pluck the string with a characteristic and particular rhythm. In Figure 7.6, you can see an example of a 332 bass—the numbers refer to the length of the notes in semiquavers. On Track 33 of the audio CD, you will hear a variant of this rhythm.

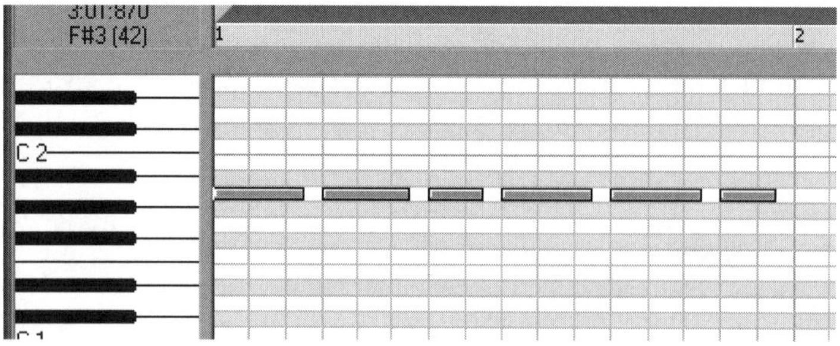

Figure 7.6   Three-three-two bassline (Track 33 on the audio CD).

And of course, any rhythm that works and complements the rhythm track can be used in this fashion.

Octave Basslines

The octave bassline pattern is an extension of the root bass in the sense that the note an octave above is also used. In a bassline that uses only roots, this represents one of the most important techniques by which a bassist can achieve some kind of variety without bringing in more notes. Like root-note playing, it is a technique that is found every-where and in every possible style of music that requires a bass. In Figure 7.7, you can see an example of an octave bassline in eighths. This type of bassline in steady quarters or eighths is sometimes called a *walking bassline*—a style of bass that is very popular in jazz, blues, rock, rhythm and blues, and many other styles.

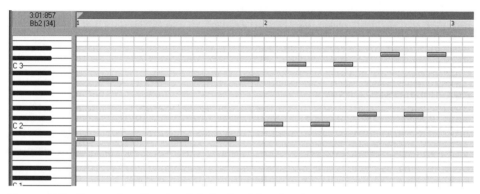

Figure 7.7   Octave bassline in eighths (walking bass).

Root and Fifth Basses

This brings us to those basslines that employ other chord tones in addition to the root. The most common kind is the root and fifth bass, which, as its name suggests, also incorporates the fifth of a chord. Queen's "Under Pressure" offers a good example of this type of bassline. After the root, the fifth is one of the most important notes of a chord. Together with the octave, it represents another way of achieving variety within the cover of a particular chord.

Root and fifth basses are universal, and they can range from the comic Tubby the Tuba and polka type of basses to the more intricate, patterned basslines involving fifth and octave (see Figure 7.8). Because this kind of bassline does not use the third, it can be used to cover either a major or a minor triad.

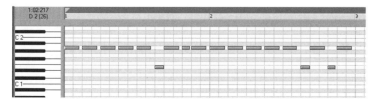

Figure 7.8   Root and fifth bassline.

Triadic Basses

A triadic bassline is one that uses all three notes of the triad in whatever order or rhythm seems appropriate for the setting. In the case of the A minor triad, which is serving as a model for our basses, this means the inclusion of all three notes A, C, and E together with their octaves (if required). See Figure 7.9.

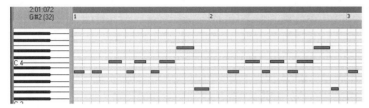

Figure 7.9   Triadic bassline (Track 34 on the audio CD).

Sixth and Seventh Chord Basses

Another very popular bass configuration involves the notes of the seventh chord, particularly the root, fifth, and minor seventh. This type of bassline is again found everywhere, particularly in jazz, blues, and rock. Examples of famous songs that use this type of bass are Santana's "Black Magic Woman" and James Brown's "Sex Machine." The sixth is also a very popular alternative to the seventh, especially with major chords, because it offers a note that can be used to add melodic interest to a bassline that otherwise only uses roots, fifths, and octaves. Marvin Gaye's "What's Going On" provides a good example of this.

Figure 7.10 shows an example of a seventh chord bassline, which in terms of our model triad of A minor, implies the chord of Am7. In this particular bass pattern, the third of the chord is also used.

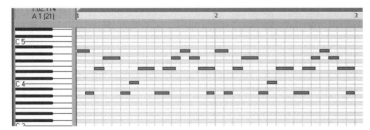

Figure 7.10   Seventh chord bassline (Track 35 on the audio CD).

Pentatonic Basslines

Bassists often use the pentatonic scale when they are playing because it offers numerous notes that can be used for decorative purposes within the range of a particular chord.

The pentatonic scale also has a peculiar magic about it in the sense that no matter what order the notes are played, they always seem to go really well together. Pentatonic improvisation is consequently one of the delights of many a bassist. In terms of our model triad of A minor, the pentatonic scale implied is the minor pentatonic, which has the notes A, C, D, E, and G (see Figure 7.11).

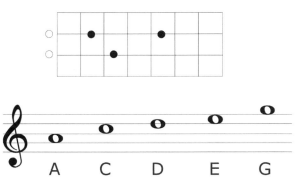

A   C   D   E   G

Figure 7.11   The minor pentatonic scale (key of A).

For more detailed information on this scale, please see Chapter 16 in *Music Theory for Computer Musicians*.

In the case of this minor pentatonic scale, the notes D and G offer decorative tones within the framework of an A minor harmony. They are called *decorative tones* because they tend to play a secondary role within the bass pattern, occurring as points of passage between the chordal tones, which in this case are A, C, and E. Figure 7.12 and Track 36 on the audio CD demonstrate an example of a pentatonic bass pattern so you can see and hear what I mean.

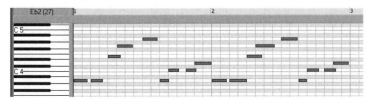

Figure 7.12   Pentatonic bass pattern (Track 36 on the audio CD).

Notice that the decorative notes D and G play a secondary role to the notes of the A minor triad. This secondary role also extends to any other notes a bassist might use to supplement the pentatonic scale. A good example of this is the sharp fourth degree of the scale, note D#, which is often used in blues scales. This is a chromatically altered note, the use of which will give a pentatonic bassline that characteristic blues feel.

They are called *secondary* notes because they are used to give the bassline a more melodic character within the cover of a particular chord. The primary notes will always be the notes belonging to the chord.

When chromatically altered notes are brought into the picture, we start to enter into the more complex and advanced territory of chromatic basslines.

Chromatic Basslines

Another way to bring more melodic interest to the bassline is through the use of chromatic notes. In the case of the scale of A minor, these would be Bb, C#, D#, F#, and G#. But they have to be used very carefully because they are not a part of the harmony. Consequently, they tend to be used as passing notes or returning tones with respect to more important chordal members. This ensures that they occur on weak parts of the measure, which means that their influence on the music remains purely melodic. One way to use them is as a fill at the end of a phrase. In the example in Figure 7.13, the previous pattern (from Figure 7.12) has been modified by adding a chromatic fill in Bar 4 (and 8).

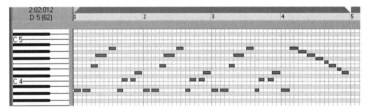

Figure 7.13   Pentatonic bassline with chromatic fill (Track 37 on the audio CD).

Another type of use of chromatic notes is as a chromatic bassline—that is, a bassline characterized by a chromatic movement of notes up or down. Figure 7.14 shows an example of a chromatic walking bassline.

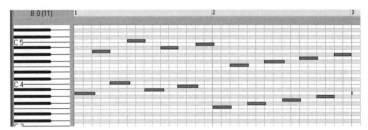

Figure 7.14   Walking chromatic bassline in eighths (Track 38 on the audio CD).

A Full Chromatic Bass Scale

Considering the different ways of bringing melodic interest to the bassline within the cover of a particular chord, it becomes apparent that starting with the root note, our review of bass patterns ended up with a full chromatic scale of 12 notes. It is this amazing spectrum of possibilities that makes bass patterns so interesting. And for the music producer, it is of course a matter of composing the right pattern for the particular situation. The diagram in Figure 7.15 summarizes the different levels of possible activity within a bassline.

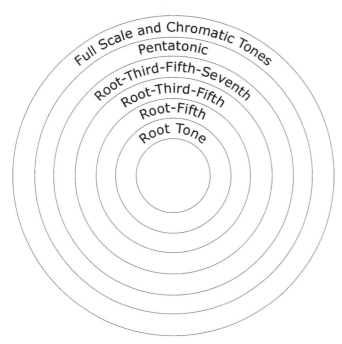

Figure 7.15 Different levels of functional bass tones.

Beginning with the root note option, the possibilities for your bassline become ever more complex and intricate as the circles widen. You will probably have some great fun exploring the possibilities of these different circles of bassline activity. It is very useful to spend time exploring these, because this will acquaint you with the different characteristic types of bass pattern, which in turn will help you when you are trying to decide what is the best type of bass pattern for your composition.

Basslines and Chord Progressions

You have seen that a bassline fulfills two essential functions. First, it offers support to the musical harmony, and second, it complements and plays a part in the rhythm track. This immediately brings us to a vitally important principle, which is that the bassline is entirely governed by the chord progression of the song. If the chord required is C major, whose notes are C, E, and G, and the bassist plays the notes E♭ and B♭, they will sound like wrong notes. Especially the Note E♭, which will clash strongly with the Note E of the C major chord. Everyone will think the bassist doesn't know what he is doing.

When you are writing your tracks, unless you are fortunate enough to have the use of a bassist, you need to think of yourself as the bassist in your ensemble. It doesn't matter how you produce the bassline. You might produce it by pencilling in the notes on your sequencer or by playing them on your MIDI keyboard and then recording them. But to be able to do so effectively, you must acquire the necessary skills that you would ordinarily expect from a bassist.

One such skill is to know in advance what chords you are going to be using in your song—which, of course, is why knowledge of musical harmony is so important. Without knowing what the chords are, although you might know what kind of bass you are looking for—a root bass or whatever—you cannot possibly know the correct notes to play in your bassline.

To overcome this obvious limitation when it comes to writing basses, another option is to create the music from the bottom up—that is, to write the bassline first and then use your ear to find the right harmonies and lead to go over it. This is an approach that many writers of dance music use. First a drum track is laid down and then a suitable bass is added. Together, these define the basic groove, which will then determine what else is added in terms of leads, pads, chords, and so on. This approach is called *groove driven*, as opposed to building a track from the lead down, which is called the *lead-driven* approach.

The order in which you compose the elements of your tracks is entirely up to you. Whether you compose it from the bottom up or from the top down, there is no fixed formula for writing a track. If the lead comes to you first, record it and then look to the process of adding a supporting bassline. And if the bass comes to you first, you can record that and then try to find a suitable lead. Although there are no fixed formulas here, there are ways of writing tracks that have been used by others and have proved themselves to be successful. And laying down a bassline after the initial step of writing a drum track is one way. Ideally, you should be able to do both—that is, be able to compose a bassline to go with the harmony and lead, or a harmony and lead to go with the bassline.

When composing a bassline with a particular chord progression in mind, there are a number of important steps to follow. Suppose, for example, that you want to create a bassline that follows the series of three simple chords shown in Figure 7.16.

| Em | Em | Em | Em | G | G/B | A | A |

Figure 7.16 Eight-bar chord progression.

First, work out the root notes involved—that is, the root progression of chords. In this case the roots are E for four bars, G for the next two bars, and A for the next two bars. In terms of a root bass, these are the notes the bassist would play. But do you want a root bass? And this brings us to the second logical step—deciding what kind of bassline you want. Having decided this, you could create a suitable bass pattern to cover your first chord of E minor.

How simple or complex the bassline turns out to be will all depend upon the musical context and what kind of bass pattern you feel would suit that context. Say, for example, that you have decided upon a root, fifth, and seventh walking bassline in eighths. In this case the first four bars would appear something like what you see in Figure 7.17.

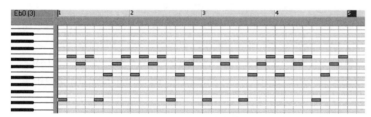

Figure 7.17 Root fifth and seventh walking bassline in eighths (E minor triad).

This pattern covers the four bars within the field of the E minor harmony. The next stage is to create a melodic extension of this pattern through the subsequent four bars. As well as representing a natural-sounding melodic extension of the first four bars, it also needs to back up the implied harmony, the chord of G major in Bar 5, G major in first inversion in Bar 6, and the chord of A major in Bars 7 and 8. One such solution would be what you see in Figure 7.18.

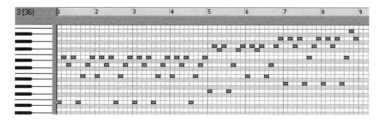

Figure 7.18 Root fifth and seventh walking bassline in eighths.

In Bar 5 the bass pattern traces the root, fifth, and seventh of the G major triad, while in Bar 6 the root is replaced with the third required for the G major first inversion triad. Bars 7 and 8 offer a continuance of that pattern within the field of the triad of A.

In this solution you can see three essential elements that define a good bassline:

1. It has a clear rhythmic identity—one that ideally complements the rhythm track (drum track).

2. It offers a clear and effective support for the harmony of the music.

3. It preserves a sense of melodic identity through all of the respective chord changes.

If you can get these three elements right, then you are well on your way toward the goal of writing effective basslines.

Synthesized Basses

In the case of synthesized basses, basic waveforms—such as processed sawtooth, square, or sine waveforms—are used either individually or in combination to replace the sounds of a conventional bass instrument. This means that when it comes to synthesized basses, you need not produce anything that sounds remotely playable. However, in actual practice, synthesized basses tend to follow the trend and patterns established through the tradition of bass playing. This is because bass players are experts at producing effective-sounding basslines. So it is not surprising that even though a bass may be synthesized, it will often use or be modeled upon an already well-established type of bass pattern.

In Figure 7.19 you can see a menu of different types of synth basses available in Logic Express.

Synth basses have become the norm in many styles of dance music and electronica in general. The type of synthesized bass that you are looking for will depend upon many features, which will include the exact style of music you are writing, the type of bassline pattern you want to produce for it, and the general role of the bassline in the mix. In drum and bass, for example, the bass to a large extent also takes on the role of a lead. Therefore, you are looking for a bass timbre that will withstand taking such a prominent role in the mix. Processed sawtooth basses, rich in harmonics, can be used effectively for this purpose. Equally, samples or direct emulations of famous bass sounds, such as the Reese bass taken from Kevin Saunderson's '80s track "Just Want Another Chance" might be more appropriate. Suffice it to say, familiarity with and extensive research of your own genre will to a large extent influence your decisions with regard to a suitable choice of bass patch.

02 Electric Bass ▶	Mini Square fat
Advanced FM	Mini Square legato
Bass + SQ	Minitune Bass
Deep Bass	Noise Bass
Dirty FM	Nordbass C
Dyn DX Bass	Octave saw shortTB
Fat Sync Bass	Octave saw TB
FB LAtt Bass	Pro Bass 1
FM Puls Bass	Pro Bass 2
FM Punch Bass	Pro Bass 3
Hard Pluck Drive	Pro Bass 4
JP8 OffBass	Pulsone Bass
JP8 UniSQ	Pulsone SQ
Klick Bass	Pulstwo Punch
Mini A basic	Pulstwo TB
Mini A dark Porta	PWM Soft Bass
Mini A dark	PWM Dark Bass
Mini A Pitch	PWM Hard Bass
Mini A short	PWM Medium Bass
Mini D basic	PWM Velo Bass
Mini Pulse Bass	Rezz Off Bass
Mini Saw Bass	Saw Legato
Mini Square Attack + Stop	Sawline 12dB

Figure 7.19 Selection menu of some synth basses in Logic Express.

Synth basses can be played and recorded at the keyboard. Their effectiveness can very much depend upon the producer's own keyboard skills. However, some of the earliest producers of electronic music soon caught on to the fact that the arpeggiators that came with their synths could easily be used to produce basslines with a degree of accuracy, rapidity of execution, and figurative agility way beyond what they could achieve themselves by playing and recording a bass at the keyboard. From this practice the phenomenon of the step-bass was born—an arpeggiating bass pattern of a certain fixed number of steps that tend to be repeated and looped through the composition.

This technology really took off with the development of Roland's famous TB-303 Bassline synth (1982), which was originally designed as a hardware instrument that could provide a bassline that guitarists could practice to. However, electronic music producers soon found that it could be programmed to produce really effective step-basses that worked well in the emerging house styles of music in the late '80s. Through such use, the characteristic acid-style bass as used in house music of the time emerged. Doepfer's MS-404, Syntecno's TeeBee, and Roland's MC-303 Groovebox were similar devices subsequently developed for the same purpose.

In the late '90s, software versions of this kind of device started to appear, such as the ReBirth program by Propellerhead, which was designed to emulate the TB-303 Bassline and the TB-808 and TB-909 Drum machines all within one package (see Figure 7.20).

Figure 7.20   Propellerhead's ReBirth (1997).

Although Propellerhead eventually abandoned the ReBirth program, some of its features re-emerged in the Reason program in the form of the Matrix Pattern Sequencer, which could be used to program step-basses and sequences, and the Redrum Drum Machine already discussed in Chapter 3.

To write effective step-basses, it becomes necessary to translate everything known about effective bassline playing into the terms of whatever device or arpeggiator is being used. This is why it is necessary to discuss synth basses separately from acoustic and electric basses, because although the underlying compositional principles are the same, the essential means of their production is characteristically different. To produce such basses on what is in effect a bass-playing machine, it is necessary to program in certain features relating to the parameters that such devices allow. The five most common of these are:

- The *note resolution* of each step of the bass pattern

- The *number* of steps in the bass pattern

- The precise *pitch* of each step
- The *velocity* of each step
- The *gate* of each step

The note resolution concerns the length of the note of each step, whether this be a quarter, eighth, or sixteenth note, and so on. The number of steps represents how many of these notes are included in the pattern. Reason's Matrix Pattern Sequencer, for example, permits a maximum of 32 steps (see Figure 7.21).

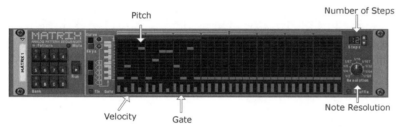

Figure 7.21 The Matrix Pattern Sequencer.

Once these have been used up, the pattern returns to the beginning and repeats. Therefore, a one-bar pattern with a note resolution of sixteenths will have 16 steps, and so on. The pattern depicted in Figure 7.21 has 12 such steps.

The pitch of each step concerns the actual note triggered, while the velocity concerns its relative volume. Finally, the gate determines how long the note will sound relative to its programmed resolution. Therefore, a gate of 50% will sound an eighth note for exactly half of that implied time. Ideally, it should be possible to set the gate individually for each note. In the case of the matrix depicted in Figure 7.21, only two options are offered for the gate—50%, which represents the default, or 100%, which is obtained by pressing the Tie button, which you can see to the left of the word Gate on the sequencer itself.

Programming and Writing Step-Bass Patterns

Step-bass patterns have become universal for most known styles of modern electronic and dance music. So well-established have they become that they now represent a generic compositional model for the creation of basslines in these styles of music. Therefore, even if you don't use an arpeggiator to generate your bassline, it is still written in a similar way—that is, as a repeating pattern of so many steps. Should you intend to write music in these styles, it is therefore essential for you to learn the principles underlying the programming of step-basses.

Because these principles represent a clear and natural extension of the principles of traditional bassline composition, you have already learned much about this from your study of this chapter so far. At the first level there are those step-basses that simply repeat the root of whatever chord is being used. Emulating the traditional practice of root-bass playing, the note used will only change when there is a change of chordal root in the music. In hardcore, hard dance, hard trance, and other kinds of upbeat dance styles, a step-bass using a resolution of eighths has become a very popular standard. This means that the bass pattern simply repeats the same note for every single eighth of the bar.

However, this type of bass often sounds like the first, third, fifth, and seventh beats are being missed due to the characteristic effect of ducking that comes from the practice of sidechaining a compressor attached to the bass-producing device. To achieve this effect, the kick signal is fed into the sidechain inputs of the compressor. This has the effect of only activating compression when the kick drum is sounding. (See Chapter 10, "The Creative Use of FX," for more on this topic.) This practice produces that pumping effect so characteristic of that style of bass (see Figure 7.22).

Figure 7.22 Synth step-bass using eighth-note resolution (Track 39 on the audio CD).

When writing step-basses, apart from the obvious parameter of pitch to consider, there are also the important parameters of velocity and gate. Velocity determines the relative level of each step. Using velocities that emulate the natural tendencies of a bass player to emphasize or subdue certain notes leads to a more organic and natural-sounding bassline, rather than a mechanical one that sounds like it is being pumped out by a machine. The highest velocities represent those notes a bass player would accent, such as the downbeat, for example, while the lowest velocities relate to the weaker parts of the bar and the use of decorative notes within the bassline. In the example of a psy-trance step-bass shown in Figure 7.23, the velocities of the notes are all varied, and certain steps are set to a gate of 100% within the Matrix Pattern Sequencer.

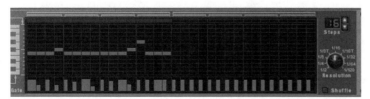

Figure 7.23 Psy-trance step-bass (Track 40 on the audio CD).

The change in the timbre of the bass that you can hear through the course of the passage is due to the gradual raising of the filter frequency cut-off of the synthesizer producing the bass sound, a common effect used with this acid type of bassline.

Any of the generic types of bass discussed earlier in this chapter can be configured and adapted into a step-bass format. A good example is a walking bass pattern, which in Figure 7.24 has been adapted for the purposes of an electro-bassline. The pattern has 16 steps, and resolution is set to an eighth, turning it into a two-bar pattern.

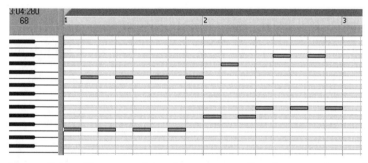

Figure 7.24   Electro walking bass pattern (Track 41 on the audio CD).

Sub-Basses

In some of the bass-driven styles of music, such as drum and bass, bassline house, and some styles of hip-hop, a sub-bass is often used. The principle of a sub-bass has been used for a long time in classical music, where the double basses often replicate the bass-line played by the cello an octave lower, or the tuba doubles the trombones an octave lower. In terms of orchestral music, this doubling of the bass in octaves greatly improves its strength and ability to offer harmonic support for all of the other instruments of the orchestra.

In electronic music the principle is basically the same—a sub-bass typically duplicates the ordinary bassline an octave lower. Timbres suitable for use as sub-basses in electronic music are those that have few or virtually no harmonics. If you select a sub-bass patch on your synthesizer, don't be surprised if you can hardly hear it. Typically, sub-basses are simply sine waveforms that have no real character. The reason for this is that a sub-bass is not actually meant to be heard, but more physically felt. It is consequently the presence of the sub-basses in a large space, such as a club, that causes such a powerful physical response to the bassline. Once you understand the principle of a sub-bass, writing for it is easy because you simply duplicate your bassline in the octave below.

Writing Basses: A Simple Strategy

In this chapter we covered much ground, making it useful at this stage to try to briefly summarize the process of writing and composing a bassline into a number of simple steps.

1. Select a bass patch suitable for the style of music.

2. If you are composing your bassline first (following the groove-driven approach), select a key and a mode in which the music is going to be written—for example, key of A, the major mode, key of G, the Dorian mode, and so on. If you are composing the bassline to fit in with the lead and harmonies, ascertain the key and mode of the music and the chord progression. This will guide you as to the appropriate notes to use in your bassline.

3. Locate the root notes of each chord and log where the chord changes are.

4. Compose a pattern that covers your first chord. Use the root note as the guiding tone around which you explore your ideas.

5. Extend the pattern to accommodate the changes of chord.

6. Edit the pattern in terms of quantization and the application of any required grooves. If your drums use a groove, then your bass should follow.

7. Apply any processing or FX required—changes in filter frequency or resonance, for example.

Conclusion

This chapter has tried to show that the principles of writing basslines have not changed very much despite changes in the means of their production. At heart, a producer of electronic music is dealing with the same essential problems as a composer of classical music in the 17th century: Does the bassline support the harmony properly? Does it have its own clear and discrete melodic identity? Does it move the music forward? Such are some of the basic questions you need to answer if the bassline is to work as a proper musical identity.

Considerations such as the aforementioned ones apply before issues of style come into the picture. When style is brought into the picture, the composer and producer are lucky to be able to draw upon the knowledge and expertise of bass players who, within the range of their own styles, have set up certain generic norms and patterns of bass playing. Learning these norms gives the producer considerable skill and latitude when it comes to the process of composing basslines. These norms also apply in terms of the process of writing synthesized basslines within the province of electronic and dance music. The difference again lies in the means of production of the bass, which is often some kind of arpeggiating device whose parameters need to be carefully studied and controlled in order to be able to produce effective basslines.

Having considered the issue of composing basslines, it is now time to consider a strongly related area, and that is the issue of the lead or main melody of a track. In doing so, we will further discuss and reference the bassline, simply because the effectiveness of the track in terms of its musical content will very much depend upon a successful relationship between the lead and the bass.

8 Writing Melodic Leads

The brief of this particular chapter is to discuss the principles underlying the writing of melodic leads. The lead is the main melody of a piece of music, and it is often linked with what commercial music producers describe as the *hook*—that catchy melodic phrase or motive that appeals so strongly to our ears. The use of such hooks occurs throughout the spectrum of commercial music, and the ability to write a good hook is more or less essential for a good songwriter. Not surprisingly, it is the hook that represents the most memorable part of a music track, as well as being the feature that can secure its recognition and popularity.

Lead Instruments

Your lead melody will ordinarily be on its own track and played by a lead instrument. There are many types of lead instruments, the principle types being acoustic, electric, and synthesized. Acoustic leads include guitar, piano, flute, sitar, violin, saxophone, panpipes, harmonica, voice, harp, trumpet, vibraphone, and any other solo orchestral melody-producing instrument you can think of.

Certain lead instruments naturally have immediate stylistic connotations that you can make good use of either by exploiting them or deliberately breaking the mold. Obvious examples are the acoustic guitar, flute, and harp with folk styles; the saxophone, muted trumpet, and vibraphone with jazz and blues styles; the sitar with its connotations of Eastern music; or the shakuhachi flute with its links to Japanese Shinto ritual music.

Electric leads include the guitar, organ, electric piano, and clavinet. Choice among these instruments is diversified by the different varieties of each instrument, such as the jazz guitar, which has a significantly different type of sound than a rock electric lead guitar. And because the guitar you use will probably derive from a synthesizer or sampler patch, there are also patches that offer emulations of various guitars as processed through effects pedals to take into account. Similarly, among keyboards, the Rhodes electric piano has a unique and highly valued sound that distinguishes it from a Wurlitzer.

Synthesized leads are many and various, and they come in a huge number of different varieties, many of which are again linked to certain styles. The huge saw lead of epic trance is a fine example, as also is the sine-wave lead so popular in hip-hop. Consequently, the choice of a lead synth patch comes very much down to style coupled with what you can hear for the lead in your own mind. Here it is very important that if you can hear a particular sound in your mind, you put in whatever efforts are needed to find that exact sound.

Ideally, a suitable lead synth sound needs to have sufficient presence to carry it over the mix. For this reason it is often processed with a large amount of reverb together with stereo delay to give the sound the fullness required of it. Mostly lead synth patches are monophonic—that is, only capable of producing one note at a time. This is a desirable quality because it produces a clean, articulated sound due to the fact that as soon as another note is triggered, it cuts off the signal to the previous note, preventing any overlap between sounds. This also enables the expressive use of portamento, which is where the notes gradually slide into one another.

When writing a lead, the quality of expression you give to it needs very careful thought. In classical music there is the piece of music being played, and there is the performer who plays it. The performer's job is to bring the music to life, to give the music that individual quality of personal expression. Writing leads using synthesizers is exactly the same. There are the notes triggered by the synthesizer to produce the melody. Then there are the expressive gestures given to them through your control of the various parameters of the synthesized sound. The quality of portamento, already mentioned, is often a strong feature of a good expressive lead, because it emulates the kind of expressive gestures used by live lead players. Most synthesizers have a control that enables you to define the degree of portamento used.

Pitch slides are another feature that belong in this category. Live lead players often employ slight pitch bends, again as an expressive gesture. Yet another quality that you might find used expressively on a lead is vibrato, which is slight fluctuations of pitch in the note caused by the way in which the performer plays it. This effect is usually achieved through manipulating the LFO—the low-frequency oscillators of the synth.

Through the use of features such as portamento, vibrato, and pitch slides, it is possible to breathe life and expression into a melody. The main melody is, after all, the lead sound, and as a lead it needs to be highly expressive. So when you load up a lead synth patch, experiment thoroughly with the various controls the synthesizer has on board. These are the tools you have to create an expressive rendition of your melodic lead. By manipulating these controls, you can bring some amazing expressive qualities to your lead so that it seems as if the lead itself is actually speaking or singing.

Melody

Whatever instrument you choose for your lead, it will be used to play a melody. Melody has always represented the very soul of music the world over. All cultures and peoples have an intrinsic love for what they regard to be a good melody. And this is not surprising in any way. There is something about melody that is capable of deeply stirring us and evoking within us emotions that can be very powerful. Joy, grief, sadness, hope, dejection—any and all of the emotions that we are capable of feeling as human beings can be stirred through melody. In this respect, melody represents the very life force of music, the common ingredient that links all of the different types of music of the world, now and in every previous age. There can be no denying that in this respect, melody is a very powerful force.

Therefore, the most important feature of a good lead line is that it needs to be melodic—that is, it needs to have the recognizable qualities of a melody. This may seem obvious, yet to be able to create melodic lines with any degree of craft and skill, you must first develop a thorough understanding of what actually makes a good melody.

The main characteristic of melody is that it is a line created through the succession of musical notes or tones. As a line, it has its own discrete identity over and above the simple sum of the notes from which it is made up. This identity is what gives melody its charm and its magic, and it is the quality by which we are able to recognize and remember the melody. It is also what allows us to distinguish between a good and a bad melody. The good melody has something about it that appeals to us—it has a polished, crafted construction, and each note plays an essential part in it. So let us look now at some of the features that give melody this quality.

Key

An aimless succession of tones, such as a random generator might produce, means very little to us. This is because good melodies tend to be clearly centered—that is, they have a strong center of gravity to them. Like the sun at the heart of the solar system or the atomic nucleus at the center of the electron cloud, this center of gravity holds the melody together and gives it a sense of direction, identity, and purpose. The musical term for this centralizing force is *tonality*, a force that becomes manifest in the note called the *tonic note*.

The tonic represents the still center around which the other notes of the melody tend to circle. The parallel to the tonic note in philosophy is the *principle*—that is, the main idea around which an argument is crafted. Consequently, a melody without a clear tonic is like an aimless, rambling argument that goes nowhere. You can hear the tonic clearly in this example of a string melody in which the tonic is sounded as a bass drone throughout (see Figure 8.1 and listen to Track 42 on the audio CD).

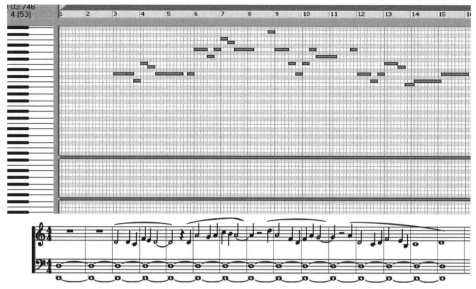

Figure 8.1 String melody with bass drone (Track 42 on the audio CD).

Listening to this tonic drone, you can see how important the tonic note is in providing a center of gravity for the music. Also notice the way in which the melody starts off with the tonic, rises upward through the scale as it acquires energy and impetus, and then gradually works its way back toward the tonic. In this sense the melody is just like an organic process. It begins slowly, acquires a momentum, and gradually falls back again to a state of quiet repose. The tonic note is that very point of repose.

To write a good melody, the first thing you need to decide is the note that will perform the function of a tonic. In this respect, any of the 12 notes of the chromatic scale defined by the keyboard can act as the chosen tonic. In the example in Figure 8.1, the tonic note is D. When performing the function of a tonic in this way, that note is called the *key-note*, and the music is said to be in that particular key. So if your chosen tonic is D, as in the example in Figure 8.1, the music is said to be in the key of D. There are therefore 12 choices with regard to the key of the music you write (see Figure 8.2).

Note: Sometimes some of the keys served by the black keys of the keyboard are described by enharmonically equivalent terms. What I mean by this it that the same black key can be named in two different ways. So the key of F# can also be described as the key of G♭, the key of D♭ can be described as the key of C#, and so on. For more information on keys see *Music Theory for Computer Musicians*, Chapter 15, "Expanding Your Knowledge of Keys."

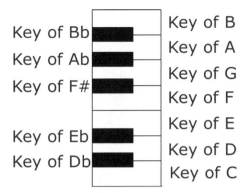

Figure 8.2 The 12 keynotes.

Scale and Mode

Another important feature of melody is the scale in which it is written. Given that a particular note has been chosen to be the tonic, the next thing to decide is the scale in which the melody will be written. The keyboard has a range of 12 notes, and it is very rare to find tonal melodies that use all 12. Melodies generally use a selection of five (pentatonic), six (hexatonic), seven (heptatonic), or sometimes eight (octatonic) notes of the 12-note chromatic scale. These notes are selected with reference to the chosen tonic, which for convenience is described as the *degree I* or the *first degree* of the scale. This description offers recognition of the importance of the tonic as the principle degree of the scale.

The choice of scale will largely be determined by the exact mood that you have in mind for the track (see Figure 8.3). A major scale will give you bright and upbeat melodies, while a minor scale will give you darker and more somber blues-type melodies. Other scales, such as the Dorian and the Mixolydian, offer a nice gradation of shades between these two. Similarly, a pentatonic scale will create a folk type of flavor, while a Spanish Phrygian scale will immediately suggest the atmosphere and flavor of the country of its origins.

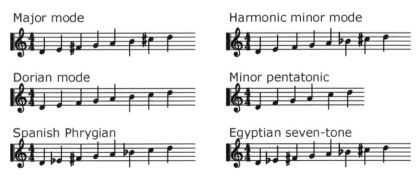

Figure 8.3 Some scales suitable for melodic composition (all in the key of D).

Ideally, you should have the freedom to use any type of scale in any key. Although it might be much easier and very tempting to learn just one key and use it for all of your songs you will regret this later. Different keys create different kinds of mood and atmosphere, and your music will greatly benefit from being able to call upon this resource. The reason why keys possess this property is unknown, and it is entirely possible that much of it is subjective. Be that as it may, for many musicians keys provide an important palette of musical atmospheres, associations, and feelings.

To get to know the scales in all of these keys, you must learn them by playing them. Having done this, it is then a relatively easy matter to pick out the salient harmonies that you would like to use within that particular scale. Most popular music is in the major or minor scale for the simple reason that they are the scales that are best known to us. Other modal scales, such as the Dorian or the Phrygian, are used as a refreshing alternative to the major and minor scales, as is the pentatonic scale. The pentatonic scale, especially in the minor form, has a strong link to blues, and therefore would obviously provide a good starting point for a composition that references this particular style. Just think of Gershwin's song "Summertime," and you will get the picture. Exotic scales, although perhaps the least used, can nonetheless offer your music a refreshing burst of exotic appeal.

Tonic and Dominant

Once you have chosen a key and a suitable scale to work with, the next thing to take into account is the tonic and the dominant relationships within that scale. The dominant is the fifth degree of the major or minor scale, which means that if you are writing in the key of C, the dominant will be the note G, whereas if you are writing in the key of E, the dominant will be note B. Tonic and dominant are related to each other as a polarity, very much like the polarity that was discussed earlier with reference to drumming—the polarity between the bass drum and the snare.

This polarity between the tonic and the dominant will provide you with the essential backbone of the melody, that central stabilizing axis around which the melody can be built. The tonic note is the point of repose in the melody, which means that it is the note that usually brings melodic phrases to a close. For this reason, it is sometimes called the *home note*. The dominant, on the other hand, is the pole of activity around which the melody tends to circle before it returns back to the tonic. In this way, ideally a melody should represent a natural and graceful series of curves that weave their way around this tonic-dominant axis. This kind of pattern probably originated with the natural melodic character of human speech. If you listen to the way people talk, you will often hear a similar pattern in the rise and fall of the pitch of their voice. They will start the sentence on a low note and then rise upward. As the sentence comes to a close, they will then fall back down again to the original note. Good melodies tend to emulate this kind of natural rise and fall that we associate with speech. Indeed, this is just like the tonic and dominant axis of a melody.

It is probably a lot easier to look at some examples in order to demonstrate this point. In Figure 8.4, you can see one of the most famous melodies in the world, the melody Beethoven uses in the finale of his Ninth Symphony, the "Ode to Joy."

Figure 8.4   Beethoven's "Ode to Joy."

This melody is useful to look at because it is entirely defined by the dominant and tonic axis as represented by the notes of C (tonic) and G (dominant) of the C major scale in which the melody is written. In the first bar the melody rises up to the dominant and then gently falls back again toward the tonic in Bar 3. The melody then gradually works its way back up toward the dominant in Bar 5, to land up gently resting on the tonic in the final bar.

From this you can see that when it is not heading toward the dominant, the melody is returning toward the tonic, and when not heading toward the tonic, the melody is heading toward the dominant. In this way the tonic and dominant relationship provides the central axis that gives the melody direction, structure, and coherence.

Another useful example to look at—a more modern example this time—is the melody of The Beatles' "Eleanor Rigby," which represents a beautiful example of melodic craftsmanship (see Figure 8.5).

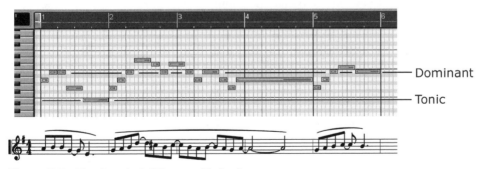

Figure 8.5   The Beatles' "Eleanor Rigby."

The tonic and dominant notes have been marked out in the piano roll view. Observe that the rising and falling of the melodic line all occur with reference to that important tonic-dominant axis. And you will notice that the dominant is the degree of the scale upon which the melody touches most often. Hence its very apt name: the dominant.

The importance of this principle for melody writing is that once you have chosen a particular scale to work with, your primary orientation will be toward the tonic and dominant degrees—the other notes of the scale representing points of passage between them. You can see this clearly in the Dorian scale of the key of E used in "Eleanor Rigby" (see Figure 8.6).

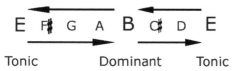

Tonic   Dominant   Tonic

Figure 8.6 Tonic and dominant poles in the Dorian mode.

In actual practice, this means simply improvising with the scale you have chosen while maintaining an awareness of the tonic and dominant degrees. Generally, a melody will start with the tonic or one of the notes of the tonic triad, head up toward the dominant and circle around it, and then gradually make its way back toward the tonic. This, however, should not be regarded as a rule. There is only one rule in modern music: If it works for your ear, go for it.

Steps and Leaps

Like the terms *kick* and *snare* with reference to drumming, *tonic* and *dominant* refer to the important functional tones of a melody. Having grasped the nature of those functional elements, the next point to consider is that all melodies are simply a combination of two things: steps and leaps. A step is a movement from one note of the scale to the next note above or below. These are illustrated in Figure 8.7.

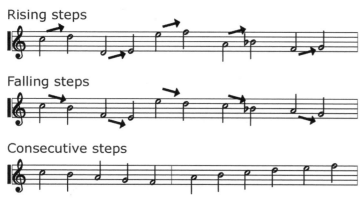

Figure 8.7 Rising, falling, and consecutive melodic steps.

To play a scale on the keyboard is to play a series of melodic steps. Because a step is a movement to the next closest note in the scale, the step tends to have a sense of smoothness and ease about it. It is strolling rather than running. Singers tend to find it easiest to sing in steps. This is because not much energy or thought needs to be given to rise or fall by just one note of the scale. A series of consecutive steps consequently has a nice, natural, free-flowing quality about it. Steps offer a melodic line its smoothness, flow, grace, and continuity. They impart to it a nice natural curvature, like a series of gently undulating hills. You can see this in the melody example first given in Figure 8.1. The steps in the melody have been bracketed in Figure 8.8.

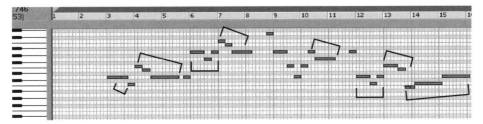

Figure 8.8 Stepwise melodic movement.

There are only two directions in which steps can go: They can rise or they can fall. Both of these relate to the emotional dynamics of melody—that is, how a melodic line is capable of affecting us emotionally. Rising steps generally speak of an intensification of energy, of a movement upward toward the realms of our aspirations.

There is a strong logic in this in the sense that rising steps are a movement from lower to higher frequencies, and therefore a movement toward energy that is vibrating more intensely and rapidly. In emotional terms, this is directly analogous to a state of excitement and arousal.

Falling steps, on the other hand, speak of a relaxation of energy, a resolution or movement back toward a state of normality. Depression and dejection are often portrayed melodically by a series of descending steps. This is because falling steps represent energy that is slowing down and vibrating less intensely. It is a falling away from the direction of one's hopes and aspirations.

All melodies use both rising and falling steps. However, a melody that was composed purely of steps would soon start to annoy us because it would sound like somebody aimlessly running up and down the stairs. This kind of melody is just a scale, really—it is uninteresting to us. As a contrast to steps, there are leaps. Leaps are movements up or down two steps or more. In Figure 8.9, you can see the leaps bracketed in the melody originally given in Figure 8.1.

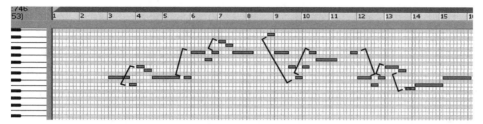

Figure 8.9 Leaping melodic movements.

Leaps give a melody energy, interest, character, and definition. They are exciting, speaking emotionally of sudden bursts of energy or sudden changes in pace. However, if a melody were composed purely of leaps, the leaps themselves would become the norm, and in so doing they would lose their power of contrast with steps. A melody like this would sound as if it were leaping erratically all over the place and, as with continual stepwise motion, we would soon lose interest in it.

Ideally, therefore, a good melody has a carefully crafted balance of leaps and steps. A further factor to consider is that leaps and steps are generally reactive to one another in particular ways. A large leap in one direction often tends to be counterbalanced by a number of steps in the opposite direction, while a number of steps in one direction often tends to be counterbalanced by a leap in the opposite direction. Figure 8.10 shows some examples of this.

Figure 8.10 Counterbalancing tendencies of melodic forces.

Note that I say "tends to be." This is because I am not speaking of rules, but of general observations. And don't just take my word for it. Study as many different melodies as you can, and you will gradually begin to see these tendencies for yourself. Again, they are very logical in terms of the emotional dynamics of melody. In nature, every action has an equal and opposite reaction. After a sudden burst of excitement (a rising leap), we tend to slowly wind down toward a normal state again (a series of steps in the opposite direction), while after a sudden shock or jolt (a falling leap), we tend to slowly recover our composure (a series of steps in the opposite direction), and so on.

In Figure 8.11 you can see these counterbalancing movements highlighted in the melody used in the last example.

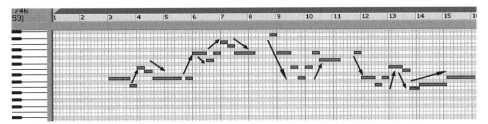

Figure 8.11   Counterbalancing of leaps and steps.

Leaps and steps consequently give you much to think about when crafting your melodies. The primary concern is always getting that balance right between rising and falling leaps and steps.

Melodic Structure

A note is the smallest event in a melody. Each such event is itself part of a larger unit or structure. A melody as a whole will represent a sum of such units. This is rather similar to the way in which letters make up words, which make up phrases, which make sentences, and so on.

The smallest structural unit in a melody is the motive. A melodic motive is characterized by two things: rhythm and pitch. The rhythm of a motive is the feature that gives it a clear and unambiguous identity. It is the motor that drives the melody forward. You can appreciate this in Figure 8.12, which plays the rhythmic motive used by Holst as a rhythmic figure in "Mars, the God of War" movement of his *The Planets Suite*. In the audio example on Track 43 of the CD, it is played on snares to emphasize its character and clear rhythmic identity.

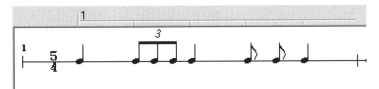

Figure 8.12   Rhythmic motive from "Mars," from Holst's *The Planets Suite* (Track 43 on the audio CD).

This is a strong and strident rhythmic motive. And you can see why Holst used it in the "Mars" movement, because it has a clear military vigor despite its unusual 5/4 time signature.

When a motive of this kind is combined with the element of pitch, then you will have an ingredient that can be used for melodic composition. Naturally, any motive that has a clear rhythm can be used for this purpose. A common technique for melody building in hard dance, hardcore, and hard trance is to first create a strong driving rhythmic motive, and second, apply that motive to various pitches of the scale.

You can see a simple example of this in Figure 8.13, in which a motive is applied to the rising notes of a minor scale. Notice that the two-bar melody starts on the tonic and rises stepwise up to the dominant note G. This stepwise rise is then counterbalanced by a leap in the opposite direction from dominant back to tonic at the end of the phrase. At the top of the figure you will see the motive itself and the fact that it has been repeated four times. Next you will see that it has been applied to the first few notes of the C minor scale. Rising upwards in stepwise motion, this creates a sense of increasing energy and excitement.

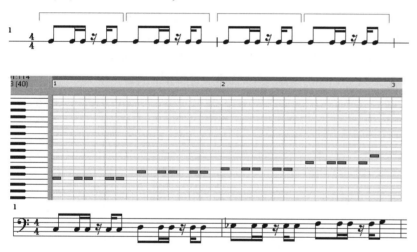

Figure 8.13 Rhythmic motive applied to rising scale (Track 44 on the audio CD).

A sequence of motives like this is called a *phrase*, and melodies tend to be built up into phrases that are then combined into larger structures, which are traditionally called *themes* (see Figure 8.14). In this way, the composition of a melodic line is often quite methodical, in that the chosen notes are first arranged into a particular motive. The motive is then repeated or varied in order to build up a phrase. Phrases are then arranged into the more substantial structural units called themes.

Figure 8.14 Structure makeup of musical themes.

This is why a melody is often said to be *crafted*. Like building a house up from the foundations, a melody is often carefully constructed from its component elements.

Fast Track to Melody Writing

If you are new to writing melodic leads, you might find the following series of logical steps helpful.

1.   Choose a key in which to work.

2.   Choose a suitable scale/mode with which to work.

3.   Play the scale through, sing it, get to know it, and log the tonic and dominant degrees.

4.   Improvise with the scale, looking out for suitable motives.

5.   Create a suitable motive.

6.   Connect different versions or variations of the motive together to form a phrase.

7.   Build up the phrases into a whole theme.

Conclusion

This chapter has endeavored to show you that to be able to write a melodic lead, it is very useful to have an appreciation of the various forces at work in melodies in general. I showed you that melodies tend to be written in a particular key, and that the keynote that defines the key performs the very important function of the tonic—the general center of gravity around which a melodic lead is built.

As well as key, we discussed the importance of a musical scale in the general sense, the scale being simply an array of pitches from which the notes used in a melodic lead might be selected. We briefly discussed a variety of such scales. The next issue we considered was the important functional tones of the tonic and dominant, which collectively form an essential axis around which the notes of a melody tend to weave themselves. We looked at some examples to highlight this point.

As well as maintaining an awareness of these functional tones within the chosen scale, we discussed the importance of creating a dynamic balance between leaps and steps. Viewed from the perspective of the emotional dynamics by which melody communicates to us, leaps and steps were shown to be essential features and considerations of a well-crafted melodic lead. Finally, we considered the matter of structure and how melodies in general have a structure that is built up gradually from the smallest components to the largest.

Significantly, we considered the issue of leads as an independent concern—that is, outside of its relationship to other functional parts of a composition. The reason for this is that melody can exist independently of other musical ingredients. A good melody can stand on its own without the support of a rhythm track, a bass, or a harmony. It seems reasonable, therefore, to consider melody independently of these other ingredients in the first instance, because this way it is possible to appreciate the forces that are at work in the process of melodic composition.

Having considered these, it is now time to look at the way in which leads, basses, and other such melodic parts should all work together as a harmonious whole.

9 Melody, Bass, and Harmony

Most computer musicians tend to produce groove-driven music—that is, music in which the drum track is composed first, followed by the composition of a suitable bassline. Other melodic and musical parts are then added above that, including a lead melody if required. It is imperative that whatever lead is composed works with and harmonizes with the bassline. The bass represents melodic material at the low end of the spectrum—material that provides a supporting role for everything that lies above it. The lead, on the other hand, represents melodic material at the upper end of the frequency spectrum, where it represents the main foreground for listening activity.

The Importance of Musical Harmony

Between bass and lead lies a very important area of music—the harmony, the field within which both lead and bass operate. Consequently, for bass and lead to work together, they must make harmonic sense in terms of the chord progression that guides them. The whole crux of this situation can be seen in microcosm if you look at a single chord, say a triad of D major. The chord has three notes, each of which will harbor a functional significance angled around the way in which we hear the chord. The lowermost Note D will be heard as the bass, the uppermost Note A will be heard as the lead, while the middle note, in between, will be heard as a harmony fill (see Figure 9.1).

Figure 9.1 D major chord embodying bass, lead, and fill.

This one example summarizes the whole situation in which a music producer finds himself, because ideally, the lead should be heard as a separate melodic part to the bass, yet both—along with any other fill ingredients—need to make sense in terms of the harmony to which they collectively give rise.

A chord from this perspective has a very particular significance, because it is the object that creates harmony between the different parts. It is no coincidence that many songwriters begin the process of songwriting by playing a chord progression that appeals to them. From that initial chord progression, both a lead and a suitable bass will gradually coalesce in the songwriter's mind.

If you do not play a musical instrument, you are hampered in this respect. For this reason it is important that you at least learn to be able to play chords and chord progressions through on your MIDI keyboard. Like a songwriter working away with his guitar, the chord progressions will often act as a stimulus upon your creative faculties, suggesting to you suitable leads and basslines that naturally emerge out of them. If you have more skill in terms of harmony, then of course you can try things the other way around—play through a catchy motive or fragment of a tune that has occurred to you and then try to find suitable harmonies that go with it.

Melody and Bass Doubling

The simplest relationship of all between bass and melody is where the two simply double one another at a distance of one or more octaves. This requires no real skill in writing two melodic lines at the same time, since the melody is simply copying the bass and vice versa. There are situations in which you might wish to do this. If you are writing a bass-led track, for example, you might want to bring your bassline out by giving it melodic support at a higher register. In the example in Figure 9.2, the lowest part has been doubled three octaves higher in order to thicken and bring out the melodic line.

Figure 9.2 Bass part doubled three octaves higher (Track 45 on the audio CD).

As a general solution to achieving a harmonious relationship between the bass and the melody, this does not really work, because although bass and lead are in perfect harmony, they are simply copies of one another. This works in certain limited contexts, but it is not a technique that is suitable for most musical contexts.

Heterophony

Another form of doubling the bass and melody involves using a particular interval, a common interval being the perfect fifth. To do this the melody is simply duplicated a fifth lower to give the bass part. There is a type of technique called *heterophony* in which all of the melodic parts roughly follow the same line. Popular in Indonesia, the deliberate use of this technique can bring an exotic sense to the music, especially when confirmed through the use of appropriate timbres. In the example in Figure 9.3 and on Track 46 of the audio CD, you will hear this technique being applied to synthesized blocks.

Figure 9.3 Heterophonic block texture (Track 46 on the audio CD).

To write a heterophonic texture, you must create your main melodic part first and then double it however many times you feel is appropriate. Both the perfect fifth and the octave work well for doubling. Then introduce changes to the individual lines as you feel are necessary to give more interest to each individual part.

Melodic Independence

In both of the previous examples, the upper and lower parts have simply been shadowing each other. Neither of these offers a suitable general solution to achieving a harmonious relationship between bass and melody. This is because in most situations you are going to want a bass and a melody that have some degree of melodic independence. This means that the lead will have its own individual melodic character and so will the bass, yet through their harmony, they will work together. The art of interweaving different melodies like this is called *counterpoint* in the classical sense. If you are to be able to write effective bass-lead combinations, you do need a certain degree of skill, at least in terms of two-part counterpoint (the two parts in this case being bass and lead).

Homophony

The simplest form of lead-bass counterpoint is where the bass and lead have similar note values and follow the same general rhythm. When this process is also applied to the inner parts, a technical style known as *homophony* results. Homophony is often typified by textures that move forward in block chords. Popular string writing is often homophonic, and it is a type of texture that we never tire of because of its lush use of chordal harmony. Listen to the example on Track 47 of the audio CD and shown in Figure 9.4, and you will immediately grasp the essence of the homophonic style.

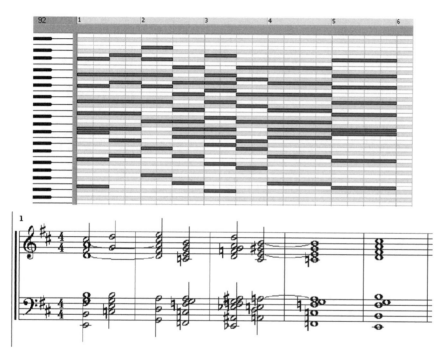

Figure 9.4 Homophonic string passage (Track 47 on the audio CD).

Notice that the uppermost and lowermost parts have virtually identical note values. Rhythmically, therefore, they are following each other, and all of the other notes between them are simply harmony notes. Looking more closely at the relationship between the upper and lower parts reveals something important about writing leads and basses. To appreciate this, the passage in Figure 9.4 has been reduced to two parts—lead line and bass—as shown in Figure 9.5.

Figure 9.5 Two-part lead and bass.

The letters refer to the type of movement between the parts. *S* stands for similar motion, which occurs when the lead and bass move in the same direction at once. *C* stands for contrary motion, which is when the lead and bass move in opposite directions. Finally, *O* stands for oblique motion, which occurs when one part remains static while the other rises or falls.

The aim of counterpoint is to create melody lines that, although running simultaneously—that is, bass and lead—nevertheless have some kind of independence from one another. Similar motion means that they are moving in the same direction. When this occurs by octaves or fifths, it sounds like heterophony, where bass and lead simply follow one another. This tends to undermine the melodic independence of the bass and the lead. Ideally, as you can see in Figure 9.5, the bass and lead are only heard to be truly independent when there is sufficient use of contrary and oblique motion—that is, the bass and lead are moving in different directions.

Putting a Bass to a Lead

This can be demonstrated more clearly by paring down to essentials and looking at some very simple and clear examples. To do this we will use the simple melody shown in Figure 9.6, played on a plain acoustic piano patch.

Figure 9.6   Simple melody in E minor.

Say, for example, that the task is to find a suitable bass for this melody. One option, which you can hear sounds very unsatisfactory, is to shadow the melody with octaves. Listen to Track 48 of the audio CD and you will see what I mean. First you will hear the melody on its own being played. Immediately following, you will hear the melody with the bassline, as given in Figure 9.7. Can you hear how ineffective it sounds just to

Figure 9.7   Melody with unsuitable octave bassline.

shadow the main melody with lower-octave notes, which are the same as you find in the melody?

Although rhythmically the bass and lead have independence, simply playing octaves of strong notes in the melody does not provide or imply a suitable harmony. A better solution is to provide bass notes that both complement the lead and give rise to a decent harmony. To do this, you must be able to read a melody and determine what kind of harmony is best for it. There are a number of simple principles that you can use to assist this process.

The first is that any melody note viewed as part of a chord can only partake in three triads. The melody given in Figure 9.6 is in E minor. The first note is E. The three chords in the key of E minor that the Note E can be a part of are E minor, C major, and A minor. There are no other triads in which the Note E figures.

E minor	E	G	B
C major	C	E	G
A minor	A	C	E

Therefore, assuming that you are looking for suitable triads, there is a choice of only three chords.

The second principle is to look at the notes of the melody and see what they imply in terms of chords. Looking at the first few notes of the melody, you can see that they trace an E minor triad, the notes F# and A appearing as passing notes: E f# G a B. For the first bar, therefore, there is really only one option: the triad of E minor. Because the melody is just starting, a root position chord is strongly implied.

Looking at the second bar, you can make similar observations. The first half of the bar traces the strong notes C and A, the notes B and G again appearing as passing notes between these chord tones: C b A g. There are only two chords in the key of E minor that use the notes A and C, and these are the chord of A minor and the chord of F# diminished. The latter chord is fairly unstable, so the best option here is the triad of A minor.

Continuing to apply this type of logic to the melody in Figure 9.6 leads to the solution shown in Figure 9.8 for a suitable bassline. You can hear this being played in the third selection on Track 48 of the audio CD.

The bassline given fulfills all of the requirements needed. It provides a strong harmony, it has contrasting note values that give it independence from the lead melody, and it uses contrary motion effectively to complement the lead—as the melody falls the bass rises

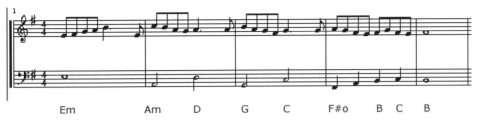

Em   Am   D   G   C   F#o   B   C   B

Figure 9.8 Melody and bass.

and vice versa. The only thing missing from this texture is a few decorative notes to give the bass some more life. Figure 9.9 shows one such solution. You can hear this as the fourth and final selection on Track 48 of the audio CD.

Figure 9.9 Melody and bass with decorative notes.

Now the bassline complements the lead at a melodic level as well. As the lead pauses with the minims (half notes) in the second half of each bar, the bass takes the opportunity to become more active. In this way the bass reinforces the melody at its weakest moments and vice versa. And to do so, it exploits a melodic figure that is present in the lead anyway, giving rise to a sense of unity and continuity. As a reminder, you can listen to these examples following each other in immediate succession on Track 48 of the audio CD in the following order.

1.   Figure 9.6: The melody on its own

2.   Figure 9.7: An unsatisfactory bassline using octaves

3.   Figure 9.8: A satisfactory bassline

4.   Figure 9.9: A bassline with decorative notes

Although this example relates primarily to classical styles of music, the principles being referred to apply to all types of music. This is because they refer to essentially musical values, as opposed to values of style or production. To make any progress in writing music in whatever style you choose to write, you must be aware of the purely musical values underlying the materials that you use in your composition. In many ways, these essentially do not change from century to century. Consequently, the songwriters of today still use the same basic chords that were used 500 years ago.

Modal Approaches to Harmonizing Bass and Lead

The approach just outlined is primarily suitable for writing in either the major or the minor scales of the key system. However, this is not the only viable approach. Some types of music do not place such a strong emphasis on tonal chord progressions. Instead, the emphasis lies on mode and color, while the harmony is more or less static. This type of harmony is typified by the use of drones and sustained notes, which provide an anchor for the main melody. As a result of the powerful influence of non-Western music upon various spheres of modern musical production, it is a type of harmony that has become very popular, occurring throughout many (if not all) styles of electronic music.

Its main popularity is due to the fact that to use a drone bass requires very little in the way of advanced musical harmony. Yet this type of static harmony offers a very powerful approach to the composition of music because it offers a certain creative freedom that is not always possible with music that uses more extensive chord progressions. Static harmony is rooted in the first instance in the use of a continuous drone or rhythmically emphasized drone note that sounds throughout the duration of the composition. An example of this was shown in Figure 9.1 (audio Track 42) if you need a reminder.

The most common type of drone is one that continually sounds the tonic note. As such, as far as basses are concerned, the drone, ground-bass, or pedal point, as it also sometimes called, offers one of the most basic types of root bass. By sounding the tonic note continuously, each note of the melody is heard as an interval with it. This interval is a type of harmony, because more than one note is sounding at the same time. The advantage of this type of harmony is that you can use any scale or mode in this fashion. Some modal scales do not offer a complete set of common triads, and in fact when you try to use them in this way, they can lose much of their character.

Figure 9.10 shows a simple example of this—the Egyptian five-tone scale, which is identical to the Phrygian mode except for the fact that the third and seventh have been missed out.

Looking at this scale with an eye to harmony, you can see that it has only two complete triads: F major and A minor. And because it does not have a complete tonic triad, the entire scale is virtually redundant as far as conventional harmony is concerned.

There are ways in which harmony in a traditional sense could be applied to it. You could use an E major or minor triad on the first degree, while there is already an F

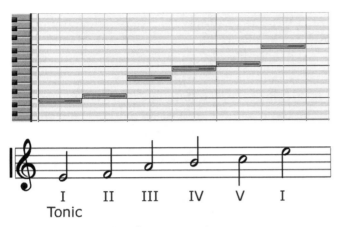

Figure 9.10   Egyptian five-tone scale.

major triad on the second. There is also a triad on the third degree, Note A—in this case, Am. The Note B poses a problem because it does not even have a perfect fifth (B-F#). So to provide a suitable common triad at this point, one of the notes of the original scale would need to be altered. The final degree, Note C, does not have a fifth, so you would need to add an additional Note G to give this note triadic support.

In this way, by endeavoring to use traditional triadic harmony within the province of this scale, the original scale itself is so severely compromised that it loses both its character and its identity. You can see this clearly in Figure 9.11, in which the alterations and additional notes required for triadic harmony have been bracketed. The original five-tone scale has now become a nine-note scale.

Figure 9.11   Alterations required to use triadic harmony with Egyptian five-tone scale.

This shows us that the Egyptian five-tone scale is not very suitable for use within the context of traditional Western harmony. Yet it is a perfect candidate for the use of static harmony—that is, the use of drones that both firmly anchor the tonic and allow the character of the scale itself to shine through. Music that does this is called *modal music* as opposed to *tonal music*. In modal music the emphasis is not so much on harmonies and changes of key, but upon melody, color, atmosphere, and mood, with each mode having its own particular *ethos* (feeling or atmosphere), as it was called in ancient Greek times.

Modal music has strong traditions in many parts of the world. A typical example of a modal music tradition is Hindustani classical music. Here a huge number of melodic modes, or *raga*, are recognized, with each raga having associated with it a particular type of mood, atmosphere, and color. A composition will typically focus upon the exploration of the properties of one particular raga. To highlight the character of the raga, drones are used that sound both the tonic and the fifth of the scale. The melody is then heard and listened to against the background of these drones.

The general purpose of modal music is to alter the mind state of the listener, to color and change their mood through the performer's skillful extemporization on the subject of the chosen mode. To accomplish this, techniques of hypnotic repetition, both melodic and percussive, are typically used. Similar techniques are commonly used in Goa trance, psy-trance, techno, house, and trance generally, because like Hindustani classical music, dance music also concerns itself with mind states. The repetitive sounding of the kick, the low throbbing of the bass, the static harmonic fields, and the continual repetition of riffs are all strong features of this musical language. Importantly, you can approach and treat any mode or scale in this fashion. The bass anchors itself around the tonic and is typically repeated in a rhythmic fashion, while the lead traces the essential notes of the modal scale. Other elements are added in to enhance the mood, feeling, and atmosphere.

Conclusion

It is very important that your bass, lead, and any other harmony fill parts work together properly to give rise to a convincing harmony. For them to be able to do this, you must at least be aware of that harmony and be able to shape them accordingly. For this reason it is often a good idea to develop a chord progression upon which to base your composition in the first place. To be able to do so, you need to learn all about chords and chord progressions and be able to play and audition them in some way that works for you. Once you have a good chord progression, the progression itself will often direct you to the choice of a suitable bass and lead. To write a bass and lead that complement one another, you also must make sure that they do not just follow each other around. The bass and lead must have a degree of melodic independence. This is achieved primarily through the directions in which they move, and secondly, through the use of contrasting note values.

10 The Creative Use of FX

Once you can write convincing drum tracks, nicely patterned basslines, and beautiful melodic leads, you are a large part of the way there in your endeavors to compose and produce your own music. The next area to consider is how to bring life, vitality, and expressive power to the sounds you use. Computer musicians often take a long time to realize that the sounds they select for use in their compositions are often simply raw material, rather than a shaped and finished product. Selecting a synth patch, they play it on the keyboard and find that it sounds lifeless and artificial. Expecting an already shaped and finished product, they are often disheartened.

The Necessity for FX

One of the most important jobs of computer musicians is to learn how to make the raw material they use sound realistic and natural. If you load, say, a piano patch to one of your modules and play a note, you will find that without FX it sounds thin and tinny. The same goes for many leads. From a lead you expect a big sound that is going to carry over the rest of the mix. Yet if you load a lead synth patch without FX, it will also sound thin.

One of your first tasks after loading a patch, therefore, is to bring the sounds to life through the use of FX. And usually this not a job to be done at the mastering stage, because if you start with thin, empty, characterless sounds, you will probably feel so dejected that you will be liable to give up the project all together. The judicious use of FX can give your sounds realism, a sense of space, ambience, depth, and presence. This, in turn, can inspire your creativity.

Natural or Endemic Effects on Acoustic Instruments

Live acoustic instruments do not use FX devices (although, of course, they may be used when such instruments are recorded). Nonetheless, there are certain natural effects that are more or less essential to the makeup and function of an acoustic instrument. Some very good examples are the reverberating chambers on guitars, drums, and stringed instruments; the loud and soft pedals on pianos; the natural echoes and reverberations arising from the space in which the music is played; the vibrations of sympathetic strings on the sitar; or those natural chorus effects arising from numerous performers singing or playing strings. These are all natural effects, which we have become accustomed to when we listen to acoustic instruments playing, and their presence makes the instruments themselves sound natural and realistic to us. This means that when we use or simulate such an instrument using software, it will sound very unnatural unless appropriate FX designed to emulate these natural effects are put in place.

Before the advent of FX devices, musicians had to go to the most incredible lengths to create certain effects. I heard a good one once where a huge gong was struck and then it was slowly lowered and lifted out of a bath of water! It both looked and sounded quite surreal. In the early days of recording studios, all sorts of ingenious methods were used to obtain particular effects. Reverb was created by constructing huge chambers with reflective surfaces, often tiled throughout. And you have probably heard of wet and dry plate effects. To obtain these, they literally had to suspend a large metal plate in a specially devised room. The effect was created when amplified sound was caused to bounce off the metal plate and then recorded by microphones placed in appropriate places. A whole roster of effects also came into being through endless experimentation with reel-to-reel tape recorders—effects such as delay, flanging, phasing, and so on. What ingenious and hard-won effects! Later, as such effects became standardized, expensive hardware FX devices came into being.

Today we are extremely lucky in that the resources eked out throughout the entire history of the development of FX devices are nearly all available to us in software forms. If we want to apply a dry plate reverb, we simply select that patch and off we go. And you have to admit that this is far easier than suspending a huge metal plate in the room! In this respect we are all very fortunate, because through the FX devices now available to us, we can convert our little home studio into a veritable alchemist's laboratory of sound. In Figure 10.1, you can see the FX menu on the left. To apply an effect, you simply double-click on it. Nothing could be easier.

Master and Insert FX

When studying FX, it is important initially to distinguish between master and insert FX. They are usually the same FX, but they perform slightly different jobs. This difference is explainable in terms of where they lie in the signal-routing process. There are master FX, which are global in their application relative to the mix, and there are insert FX, which apply their effect only to a particular device—for example, an acoustic guitar patch.

Figure 10.1 Ableton Live FX. Ableton Live is noted for its really good menu of insert FX (which is shown in the left-hand column).

Master FX

Master FX are used to affect the signal output through the L and R channels of your main mixer. They are connected to and controlled by the auxiliary returns of the mixer. The auxiliary controls on your mixer (Send and Return) enable you to determine how much of the signal is sent and returned through the auxiliaries. You can see their role in Figure 10.2, which shows the example of a piano patch routed to a particular channel of the mixer.

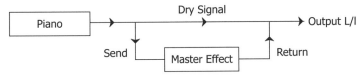

Figure 10.2 Placement of master FX in the signal-routing process.

Of all the types of FX, master FX tend to be the most standardized in that they are concerned with bringing a sense of warmth, ambience, space, and presence to your final mix. A typical combination of master FX would thus be compression, reverb, and chorus, with compression to pump up the mix, reverb to give it a sense of space, and chorus to add depth and presence. Naturally, these would be variously applied in the discrete amounts required by each particular channel.

Insert FX

Insert FX are the devices that process the signal output from a particular sound-producing device used in your composition. Figure 10.3 shows the placement of an insert effect relative to a master effect.

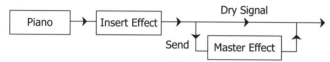

Figure 10.3 Placement of insert FX in the signal-routing process.

Because master FX perform a global role in the mix, they are often constrained by the requirements of getting the final mix sound just right. And because mixers only have a certain number of auxiliary inputs, these are often taken up with those essential FX required for this job. Insert FX, however, tend to be used much more flexibly in that their major concern is affecting the sound of only one particular device. Consequently, they offer much more scope for experimentation, originality, and creativity. A typical example of the application of an insert effect is routing the signal from a lead synth through a chorus effect in order to give it a much thicker and fuller sound. Another example is routing a conga pattern through a suitable large-room reverb to give the congas a fuller and more natural sound.

Creative Use of FX

Spend as much time as possible experimenting with and getting on intimate terms with your FX devices. The purpose of this is twofold. One, it will increase your knowledge and ability to use these FX in standard ways, which you will gradually learn about as you try to perfect your sound. And by "standard ways," I mean, for example, using FX such as reverb and delay to make a piano patch sound realistic. The second purpose is that it will assist you when you come to use your FX as a direct compositional tool.

When a composer writes a violin part for an orchestra, he does not have to bother with such things as FX devices. Consequently, these devices are not a part of the compositional process. The electronic and dance music of today is very different than this, for there you will find that FX are being used constantly to modify the basic raw material used in a composition. And this process has become such a prominent feature of the music that it now needs to be viewed and approached as a compositional ingredient that is, in its own way, just as important as melody, harmony, and rhythm.

Compression

Compression is a type of dynamic effect you can use to affect the levels (measured in terms of decibels) of a track or indeed a whole piece of music. In Figure 10.4, you can see the MClass software compressor that comes with Reason 4.0.

Figure 10.4 The MClass compressor.

The best way to understand compression is by considering a situation in which it might be required. Vocal tracks are nearly always compressed due to their relatively large dynamic range, which can extend from the loudest passionate screaming down to the quietest possible whisper. Compression allows you to balance this range out so that the loudest parts are a bit quieter and the softest parts are a bit louder. The result is a much more even level. The applications of this to drum tracks are also evident, because these also tend to have a very wide dynamic range. The threshold of the compressor is set to determine the level at which compression will kick in. Any signal that exceeds this threshold will then be compressed.

On the left of Figure 10.5, you can see the uncompressed sound of a drum track in which the crash cymbal exceeds the required threshold. On the right you can see what happens to the level of the crash once the peak signal has been compressed.

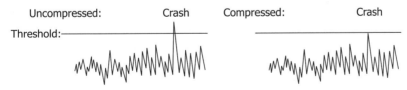

Figure 10.5 Compression of signal that exceeds the threshold.

Once the signal is compressed, you can apply gain productively to boost the overall volume of the quieter parts (see Figure 10.6).

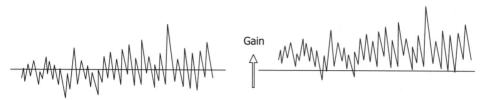

Figure 10.6 Applying gain.

This standard compression process is very useful for guitars, pianos, drum tracks, vocals, and any type of sound, in fact, that tends to have a wide dynamic range.

Side-Chaining

When a signal is routed to the side-chain inputs, this signal triggers the compressor. A typical application of this process would be an acoustic guitar part in, say, a heavy rock track. To come through in the mix, the acoustic guitar would be sidechained so that when it enters, compression will then be triggered to bring the other parts down to a level where the acoustic guitar can be clearly heard. When the acoustic guitar part stops, compression will similarly cease.

Side-chaining has been used in a more creative way to get that pumping effect characteristic of French house tracks, such as Daft Punk's "One More Time." By splitting the signal of the kick and routing it to the side-chain inputs, whenever the kick is heard, the level of the other parts reduces. The use of one signal to reduce the volume of another in this way is called *ducking*; an example of this was given in Figure 7.22 and audio Track 39 on the CD.

Reverb

Reverb concerns the reflections of sound waves from the surfaces of the enclosure in which the sound is produced. Have you ever been up in the mountains and shouted, and then heard the echoes of your shouts bouncing from cliff to cliff? This is an example of sonic reverberation. The presence of these reflections gives us a profound sense of the space in which the sound is occurring. As a result, it is through the natural effect of reverb that we can immediately tell whether a sound is coming from, say, a tiled bathroom, a cathedral, or a cave.

Reverb FX are algorithms cleverly designed to emulate this natural effect. Their discrete and proper use is an essential feature of every composition. Generally, reverb tends to be used in two ways. First of all, reverb is used to impart a sense of realism to the sounds that you use, giving the listener the impression that the sounds are coming from somewhere other than your soundcard! The salient question here is this: Do the sounds sound natural against the purpose for which they are being used? To persuade your listener that the sounds are natural, you need to bathe them in the appropriate types of reverberation. Through your use of reverb, the snare sounds like a real snare rather than just a dry sample, and the piano you are using sounds like a real piano being played in a real location.

Second, through appropriate use of reverb, you have the opportunity to create highly imaginative soundscapes that are full of atmosphere and a profound sense of space and dimension. To achieve this sense, the first question you need to ask is: What kind of space does the composition suggest? This question is answered by looking at the imaginative scene in your mind as you compose your track. Where are you? Are you on a mountaintop, in the vast emptiness of space, in a dense jungle, under the sea, or on a beautiful, exotic beach? All of these different kinds of imaginative environments have strong connotations with regard to the type of reverb associated with them. Through the correct use of reverb, you can suspend your listeners' sense of disbelief and transport them in their imagination to that particular place you have in mind. As they listen to your music, they can feel the sense of partying on the beach, journeying through the jungle, feeling the heat of the club, or whatever. In this sense reverb is not just a sound effect, but a vital compositional ingredient.

One of the silliest uses of reverb I ever heard was in a production in which the singer was singing about the intimate feelings she had for her lover. The reverb unthinkingly used was a type of stadium reverb, and although it gave the singer's voice a great sense of hugeness, it sounded ridiculous in terms of the sense of intimacy the song was trying to convey. To give a sense of intimacy, you would not automatically use a reverb that suggested a singer in the center of a stadium surrounded by 100,000 people! Suffice it to say, you must carefully think about the use of reverb in terms of the type of feelings you are trying to convey.

The knack to using reverb lies in your ability to translate what can often be quite nebulous feelings, suggestions, and atmospheres into the tangible parameters of the given reverb device. Perhaps the most important parameter is the room size. Reverb FX devices allow you to specify the size to a greater or lesser degree. What size of space does the music suggest? Where is it all happening? What is the location? A small room, a concert hall, a huge arena, a club, or a vast, empty cave? Looking at the reverb effect in Figure 10.7—the DSP-FX Studioverb (SONAR)—you can see that on the far left is a control that enables you to specify the size of enclosure from the smallest to the largest.

Coupled with the size of the enclosure are the parameters of pre-delay and decay. Pre-delay sets the time of delay of the reverberations. Naturally, the larger the space, the longer the delay between them. In this context, pre-delay can also be used to impart a sense of distance. Imagine the sound of a horn call on a distant mountain—the pre-delay would be a pretty large one.

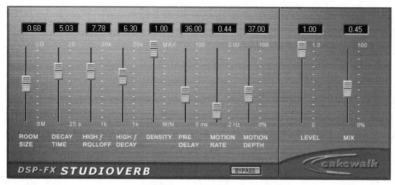

Figure 10.7 Reverb DSP-FX Studio Verb (SONAR).

Decay concerns the amount of time it takes for the reverberations to die down. Think of spaces in which the decay is a slow, gradual one—cathedrals or large underground caverns where the sound has nowhere to escape. The type of surface the sound bounces off can also affect the decay. A smooth, wet surface would have a longer decay time than a dry, porous surface.

Some reverb devices have an EQ on board that allows you to control the frequency spectrum affected by the reverb. Too much lower-frequency reverb can fill your mix with boom and muddiness, which is not really necessary for the effect. Similarly, too much high-frequency reverb can cloud the upper registers of your mix. Consequently, the EQ needs to be adjusted so that you can get the benefits of the reverb without the disadvantages of muddiness and cloudiness.

This brings us to the parameters of wet and dry defined on a scale from 0 to 127. Zero is a dry sound, unaffected by the reverb, while 127 is a totally wet sound in which the entire signal is processed by the reverb. Adjust this using your ear, taking it to the maximum possible before you start to hear unnecessary feedback. You will be able to tell this point because you can hear it when it occurs.

Reverb will undoubtedly be necessary as one of your master FX, and virtually every device on your mixer will be given some degree of reverb. Some types of kick do not tolerate reverb, whereas on others a touch of reverb works quite well. Certainly, the snare and clap will use reverb, as will the open hi-hats. The degree of reverb all depends upon the type of sound you use. A big snare sound will require plenty of reverb.

If your mixer allows it, you can use a number of reverb devices that will perform different functions. Reverb devices often give you pre-programmed options that will nearly always include drum hall reverbs, which are really effective for bringing a sense of realism to your drum tracks. Functional percussion can also be brought to life in this way. In electronic music, basses are often dry, although again it depends upon the kind of bass sound you want. A bass stab can be made to sound really effective with the right kind of reverb.

It is not necessary to think of all kinds of reverb as a fixed or static effect. Often you can obtain good results by automating the parameters of your reverb device and making changes to those parameters here and there. Alterations to the decay time can be really effective in this respect. In Figure 10.8, you will see a production trick that uses reverb decay to create entirely new sounds. A chord is played on a synth patch, and the reverb decay is set to infinite. This means that the reverberations of the sound will go on for-ever! The result is then sampled, and the attack of the chord cut off, leaving just the reverberating sound of the original chord. This sound is then brought into a sampler and treated as you would any other sample. In this case the sample has been treated by automating the semitone settings of the oscillator. You can hear the result on Track 49 of the audio CD.

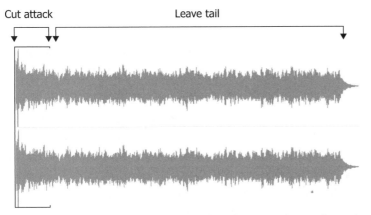

Figure 10.8 Resampled reverb tail (Track 49 on the audio CD).

By applying this little trick, you can get all sorts of amazing ambient sounds, from heav-enly sounding choirs to beautiful shimmering pad sounds.

Delay

Along with reverb, delay is one of the most widely used FX. Delay is simply the echo of a sound that occurs so many milliseconds after the original. The length of delay—as measured in milliseconds—can be precisely specified. Delay times that work best tend to be those that work with the beat, although you can obtain interesting FX by using multiples or fractions of the length of the beat. For this reason you must be able to calculate the length of the beat in terms of milliseconds. This is done by dividing the minute by the figure of the tempo as measured in beats per minute (BPM). If the tempo is 160 BPM, 60/160 = 0.375 = 375 milliseconds. Therefore, a delay time of an eighth note would be worth 187 milliseconds, and a delay time of a sixteenth 93 milliseconds, and so on. Fortunately, some delay plug-ins work out the value of fractions of the beat in milliseconds for you. The digital delay device that comes with Reason does this (see Figure 10.9).

Figure 10.9 The DDL-1 Digital Delay Line (Reason).

Feedback is the parameter that lets you specify how many repetitions of the echo occur: The greater the feedback, the greater the number of repetitions. Set to full, the repetitions would virtually continue indefinitely.

Steps is a parameter that enables you to specify the length of the delay in steps measured as a fraction of the beat. In the case shown in Figure 10.9, the resolution is set to 1/16, and the number of steps is 4. This means the delay will occur after four sixteenth notes.

Panning concerns the direction of the stereo field from which the echo comes. In Figure 10.9, the delay is panned right. Through automation, it is possible to emulate the processes of stereo delay and cross delay where the taps come from different points of the stereo field. Cross delay is where the taps cross over from left to right in the stereo field. Connecting a low-frequency oscillator to the CV panning input, it is possible to cause these taps to sweep across the stereo field in a more random type of pattern.

Delay is related to reverb through the common factor of echo. For this reason, when using delay you will probably use less reverb, or at least apply it much more sparingly. Applied liberally, it can lead to a messy sound. Instruments such as guitars and pianos benefit greatly from a touch of delay, and it is a good trick to use two delay devices as master FX, one panned left and the other panned right, set to different step parameters—say, for example, a three-step delay for the left-panned device and a four-step delay for the right-panned device. This mixture of steps and panning gives rise to a nice, thick, full, and resonant type of piano or guitar sound. Drums can also benefit from delay patterns, and through thoughtful use of delay, you can make a simple drum track sound extremely intricate and complex.

It is always well worth experimenting with delay because it can bring sounds to life in some of the most extraordinary ways. In Figure 10.10, you can see a WAV file that consists of five separate examples of delay types being applied to the same loop. You can hear these excerpts on Track 50 of the audio CD, together with an explanation of their processing as given in Figure 10.10.

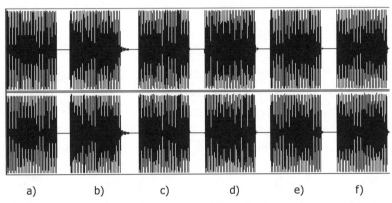

a)   b)   c)   d)   e)   f)

Figure 10.10   Different delay types—WAV diagram—Track 50 on the audio CD.

a)   In the first excerpt you will hear the loop itself, which consists of a kick and a Rhodes chord stab sample. The sample doesn't sound so good because it is simply the raw material, yet to be treated and processed.

b)   In the second excerpt you will hear a four-step delay of a simple Rhodes chord stab that has been panned to the center. A kick has been provided to give an idea of time.

c)   In the third excerpt you will hear the stab being treated with three-step delay, a significantly different type of step effect.

d)   In the fourth excerpt you will hear both a four- and a three-step delay being applied on two respective delay devices, one of which has been panned left and the other panned right. This gives a more complex delay pattern.

e)   In the fifth excerpt you will hear a four-step delay pattern, the panning of which is being controlled by a low-frequency oscillator, causing the taps to sweep between left and right within the stereo field.

f)   In the sixth and final excerpt you will hear the feedback being turned up very high, causing almost continual repetition of the echo.

Filtering

Filtering is another effect that I would never be without. It is a type of spectral effect in that it affects the harmonic frequency spectrum as a whole. Filtering is the process whereby some frequencies are allowed to pass through while others are blocked. This has a profound effect upon the perceived timbre and color of the sound being filtered. A high-pass filter lets in the high frequencies but not the lower ones. A low-pass filter lets in the lower but not the higher frequencies, while a band-pass filter lets through frequencies within a certain specified band.

Virtually all sound-producing devices you use will have a filter (or filters) on board as primary shapers of the sound. You need to play around and adjust them until you have the sound you require. As a separate insert effect, filters are generally used as tools for shaping and transforming the sound, and there are two general ways in which they can be used for this purpose. They can be used for static FX—that is, FX that do not change through time. For this purpose the sound is shaped as required and then left as it is. To obtain the required sound, you must perform much experimentation with the controls of the filter. Principally, these are the filter frequency and the filter resonance. The filter frequency determines how much of the frequency content is allowed to pass. When the higher frequencies are filtered out, the sound is characteristically darker and mellower, whereas when the lower frequencies are filtered out, the sound is much brighter but lacks body and depth. The filter resonance, in turn, causes an emphasis of those chosen frequencies.

Secondly, filters can be used for modulation FX in which parameters of the filter will change through time. The most common effect for this purpose is the filter sweep, which utilizes the filter frequency cut-off control. Rising from low to high, this has the effect of gradually allowing more and more of the frequency content through, thereby producing a characteristic transformation in the timbre of the sound from dark to very bright. This is a very common effect in all electronic and dance music, and it is used in many different ways: to cause the gradual rising to prominence of a lead or riff, to gradually introduce or alter the timbre of the drum track, or to cause a pad sound to gradually gain in brightness and intensity. To achieve these FX, the filter frequency and resonance are automated on their own respective channels.

In Figure 10.11, you can see some of the filter automation used in audio Track 51 applied to the percussion track. The drums you can hear coming in are on a band-pass filter, and the filter frequency is set to its highest point. Then, after 16 bars, the filter is suddenly disabled, allowing the drums to be heard in their fullness.

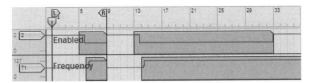

Figure 10.11 An example of filter automation.

As affecting the spectral content of a track, filtering can be used in a huge variety of ways, especially to cause gradual transformations of heard frequency content within a given track. Within loop-based music it represents one of the main tools for maintaining the listener's interest in the continually repeating looped material. This is because through the use of filtering, the focus of attention shifts from the repeated material to the filtering process itself. The secret here is to ensure that your material is never presented statically: Everything needs to be constantly shifting, modulating, and slowly transforming. Insert FX such as filtering are primary tools with which to achieve this.

Chorus

When a choir sings a melody, each individual singer produces his or her part at a slightly different pitch and phase than the other singers. This also applies to string players in a string section. This produces the effect called *chorus*—a thickening of the melodic line as a result of these slight deviations of pitch and phase between the separate performers. Chorus FX are designed to emulate this particular effect, which means that their primary use is to cause a thickening of the overall sound. When used on lead synth parts, chorus FX can give them more thickness and depth. When the rate of pitch variance is increased, the chorus acts as a detuner. In this way, you can create powerful detuned trance leads from what would otherwise just be an ordinary synth lead.

FX Chaining

By connecting the output of one insert effect to the input of another effect, you can set up FX chains through which it is possible to create extremely complex modulating sound tapestries. In Figure 10.12, you can see the principle behind FX chains.

I know of one writer of ambient music who always sends the whole mix through a huge connected chain of devices. By making changes to the parameters of such devices, you can create amazing and complex sounds from what are, in effect, very simple materials. In Track 52 on the CD, you will hear a chord that has been processed

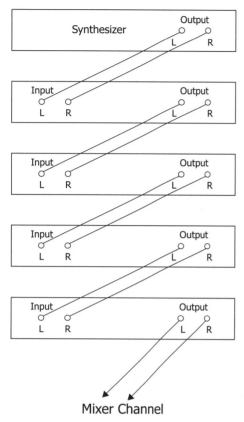

Figure 10.12 FX chaining.

through such an FX chain. As a result of the processing, the chord has acquired a shimmering, modulating depth and presence. Suffice it to say, it is well worth experimenting with FX chains.

Experimentation

There is a huge range of FX devices available, and this small chapter can do no more than scratch the surface. In Figure 10.13, you will see a spider diagram that includes some of the best-known types of devices. Even there, the number alone is sufficient to make the mind boggle.

The possibilities for the use of these devices, both individually and in combination, are infinite. For this reason the computer musician need never feel that he or she has nothing to do. If you are going through a dry patch and not writing much in the way of new material, then set up a simple loop and spend time experimenting with your FX devices.

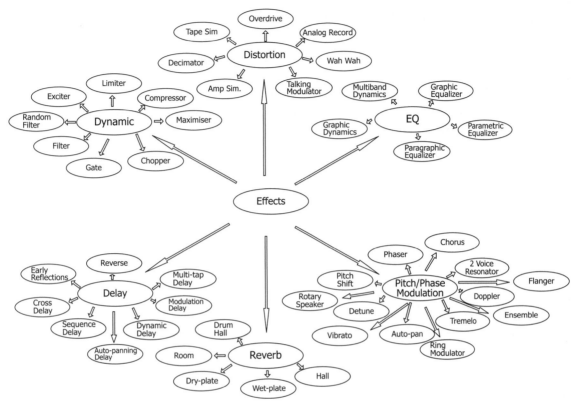

Figure 10.13   Range and types of FX devices.

Explore their parameters and see what you can achieve. Be totally creative, inventive, and outrageous with them, push them to their very limits, and explore the kinds of extreme FX that you can obtain. You never know, through your explorations you might come up with a totally new kind of sound.

Conclusion

This chapter showed that the use of FX is just as a much a creative ingredient of modern composition as other more traditional ingredients, such as drums, melodies, basses, and harmonies. For this reason, the computer musician needs to get on intimate terms with his or her FX devices and know what they are, how they affect the sound, and how can they be used to good advantage. To acquire this knowledge, you need to do a lot of experimentation, trial and error, and open-minded investigation.

You generally will use the knowledge you acquire in two essential ways. First, you'll use FX to obtain the kind of sound that you want, whether this be a grand piano, tremolo strings, or an acid bassline. You'll need to process all such instruments through suitable insert and master FX to give them life, realism, vitality, power, and presence in the mix. Second, you'll use FX creatively in order to create more interest and variety in your music, whether this be the occasional use of flanging or phasing in your drum track, the use of the filter frequency cut-off and filter resonance to create modulating basslines, or the use of distortion to add some dirt to your mix. And whatever you do, make sure that nothing is left to remain static. Through your use of FX, you can give your music constant movement, life, and a sense of forward progression.

11 Writing for Strings

S trings are one of the most popular and versatile instruments used in modern electronic music. Everybody loves the sound of strings, and unlike with some other instruments, our ears never tire of the richness, quality, and warmth of the string sound. Indeed, they have been (and still are) one of the best ways to infuse your music with warmth and emotion.

The computer musician will probably use synthesized or sampled strings, which are quite a different proposition from the real thing. Generally, there are two ways you can use these string patches. You can simply select a string patch at random and audition it to see whether it offers the string sound you are looking for. Alternatively, you can spend some time getting to know strings, how they are played, and the different kinds of sound you can get from them. I much prefer the latter approach, and although this requires some study, it nonetheless leads to a much more versatile, knowledgeable, and professional use of strings. It also helps you to understand the different types of string sounds your synth and sampler patches are trying to emulate.

Four Types of Strings

A single stringed instrument can generally be one of four different generic types. There is the violin, which represents the main lead instrument of the string family and has a range that extends from Note G2 up to about G6. Like all of the instruments of the string family, it has four strings, which in the case of the violin are tuned to G2, D3, A3, and E4. On a real violin, each string has its own particular character and signature sound, something which professional composers take into account when they are writing for the violin. You have probably heard of Bach's "Air on a G String," which represents an example of this type of violin writing, the whole solo being played on the lowermost string of the violin, which is tuned to the Note G2. When it comes to synthesized strings, though, the different characters of the four strings usually are not emulated, so you need not worry about this aspect.

After the violin comes the viola, a larger type of violin that has a deeper range, the four strings being tuned a perfect fifth below the strings of the violin—that is, to C2, G2, D3, and A3. The sound of the viola is typically heavier and darker than the sound of the violin, and it is often used as a harmony fill instrument.

Below the viola in the string range are the cellos, which along with the double-basses represent the bass instruments of the string family. The four strings of the cello are tuned an octave below the four strings of the viola, which means that it has a characteristically deeper sound. The largest members of the string family, the double-basses, are often used simply to double the cello part an octave lower (as you might expect from their name). For this purpose the strings are tuned in fourths beginning with the Note E0. This usual doubling of the cello part by the double-bass gives the bass part more body, strength, and power, qualities that are vital if the string bass is to have any presence or standing in terms of the orchestral sound as a whole. Consequently the double-basses are the "sub-basses" of the string family.

Types of String Ensemble

To provide a representative and inclusive range of string sounds, the designers and creators of synthesizer and sampler string patches have to take into account two very important parameters. First, there is the type of string ensemble, and second, there is the typical style of playing. To write effectively for strings, you need to understand and take into consideration both of these parameters. Let us first consider types of ensemble.

There is the solo stringed instrument, which is usually the violin, viola, or cello. The double-bass is not usually provided for as a solo instrument simply because it does not compare to the cello for richness and warmth of tone. Most typically in this category, you would have a solo violin and then, as a viable alternative for the lower registers, a solo cello. These two options tend to cover most requirements for the use of a solo stringed instrument. In both cases the appropriate use of reverb becomes an important consideration.

For a solo stringed instrument to have warmth, presence, and quality of tone, it needs to be given sufficient reverb. The type of reverb depends upon the context. A folk-type violin solo would naturally benefit from an outdoor type of reverb patch, whereas an emotionally charged string solo would benefit more from a hall type of reverb, emulating the space and atmosphere of the concert hall.

Another effect that proves useful in a solo context is delay, which, by contributing slight echoes of each note or phrase of the music, gives the solo instrument more depth and presence. For an example of a beautiful string solo that uses both reverb and delay, have a listen to the introduction of the track "Salva Mea" by Faithless.

The simplest main type of string ensemble is the string quartet, composed of two violins, a viola, and a cello. In classical music the string quartet is one of the perfect mediums for personal and intimate musical expression. Used in a more modern sense, it still retains this sense of personal intimacy. It is a type of string sound that tends to draw the listener in. Composed of four solo instruments, it benefits from the same type of effects setup as a solo stringed instrument.

After the string quartet there is the string ensemble, in which each of the instruments of the string quartet is at least doubled, and the double-bass is also included. This produces an ensemble sound that is quite light and sparing when compared to a full string orchestra. It is consequently suitable for musical situations in which you want a string presence, although one that is not as lush or full as the complete string orchestra. At this point you can start to bring chorus effects in to provide the necessary thickening of the overall sound. If you want to hear a string ensemble put to good use in a popular song, try listening to The Beatles' "Eleanor Rigby." This uses a double string quartet arrangement produced by George Martin.

The full string orchestra consists of at least 30 violins, 12 violas, 10 cellos, and about 8 double-basses. These numbers reflect the requirements of being able to produce a balanced tone in all registers. After the solo stringed instrument, this rich, lush, and full type of string sound, commonly associated with pieces such as Samuel Barber's "Adagio for Strings," is probably the most widely used by computer musicians. Owing to the fullness of the string orchestra sound it is particularly good for providing rich chordal backgrounds and textures. To be able to write these effectively, however, it is of course necessary to learn how to score string chords properly.

Scoring String Chords

One of the most popular uses for strings in modern and electronic music is to supply an ambient chordal background. The computer musician can learn a lot from the way in which such chords are often scored for strings by professional composers. A typical scoring of, say, a chord of C major, would be as shown in Figure 11.1.

Notice that the widest intervals in the chord are in the lower parts, and as the upper register is reached, the notes are crowded more closely together in the chord. This is because small intervals in the lower register sound muddy due to the conflicting low register harmonics. Consequently, an ideally spaced string chord would be nice and wide down low and get gradually narrower as you go up through the register. The harmonic series, if you think about, represents the natural archetype upon which this type of chordal spacing is based. This chord of nature consequently provides you with a very good guide as to the best way to score chords (see Figure 11.2).

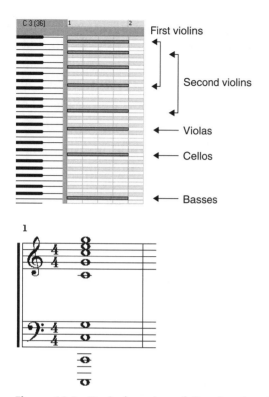

First violins

Second violins

Violas

Cellos

Basses

Figure 11.1 Typical scoring of C major chord for string orchestra.

In Figure 11.2, notice that the larger intervals occur lower down in the harmonic series and that the higher in the series you go, the more closely crowded together the notes become. Observe also that the first four harmonics give a chord of open fifths and octaves (power chord), the first six harmonics a major triad, the first seven harmonics a chord of the seventh, the first nine harmonics a chord of the ninth, and the first eleven harmonics a chord of the eleventh. Harmonics seven, eight, nine, ten, eleven, and twelve together give rise to a chord that modern classical composers refer to as a *tone cluster*—a chord composed of closely crowded notes from the same scale.

Styles of String Writing

In addition to the type of ensemble, a second important parameter to take into account when writing for strings is the style of playing. When writing for or including strings as a part of your tracks, you will have to decide what style of playing is appropriate for your needs. To be able to do this, you need to familiarize yourself with some of the generic types of string writing that professional composers and music producers use.

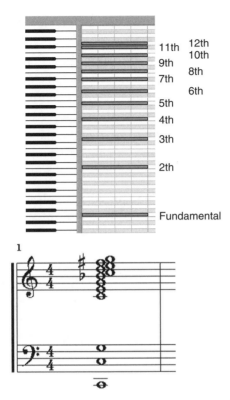

11th   12th
        10th
9th
        8th
7th
        6th

5th

4th

3th

2th

Fundamental

Figure 11.2 The harmonic series as it defines an ideally spaced chord.

Legato Strings

You can make progress in your string writing by watching the ways in which a stringed instrument is played. To create a note, the player's left hand stops the string with a finger, and the bow is drawn down over the string. Stringed instruments are fretless, which means that the player's placing of his or her finger is always an educated estimate of the exact point where the finger should be placed to produce the appropriate note. For this reason string intonation is often quite flexible.

The way the bow is drawn produces the characteristic types of string playing that you are used to hearing and are probably going to want to use and emulate at some time or another in your compositions. The most popular style of playing is legato bowing, in which there is a smooth unbroken connection between each of the notes. Occurring when the string player keeps the bow in continuous connection with the string, this kind of bowing is best imitated on samplers by the use of a long, continuous note.

This style of playing is very suitable for string solos, especially in the slower tempo range. An example of the latter can be heard on Track 42 on the CD. When emulating this type of bowing, bear in mind that with the real instrument the down-bow has a much stronger attack than the up-bow. This is because the string is played with the heel of the bow rather than the tip and therefore receives more pressure. Consequently, a string player will tend to produce notes that occur on strong points of the measure with a corresponding down-bow. To emulate this using sampled sounds, create your velocity curve with an eye to strong and weak points of the measure. Alternatively, you can try automating the amplitude envelope attack slider.

In Fatboy Slim's "Right Here, Right Now," you can hear a good example of the legato string style. In this track he uses two string parts in counterpoint with one another, a melody and a countermelody that go together well and produce a great feeling of drive.

Another common use of legato strings in electronic music is as a pad type of sound. The string sound is particularly rich in harmonics and generally produces one of the best pad sounds there is. Being rich in harmonics, filtering can be used to great effect. When using strings as a pad, they supply a background warmth and ambience to the track. This kind of legato string writing mostly uses long sustained tones that change with the harmony. A useful trick to bind the whole sound together is to tie notes that successive chords have in common. This helps to create that smooth, unbroken connection between successive chords of the chord progression. You can see this technique being used in Figure 11.3.

Because the top note F# is common to all four of the chords that figure in this chord progression, it is simply tied throughout the whole passage. At every other point where successive chords have a note in common, this note is also tied over, ensuring a smooth, audible connection between successive chords.

Pizzicato Strings

After legato bowing, another very popular type of string sound is pizzicato strings. Here the bow is not used to play the notes as the string is simply plucked with the finger, like the string of a guitar. Unlike a guitar string, however, this produces a short, crisp sound that you can use to great effect in some passages. This style of playing is perhaps best known in jazz, where it represents the characteristic way of playing the double-bass. Rather than being bowed, each bass note is produced by plucking the appropriate string.

When the entire ensemble plays, pizzicato chords can be played. These have a crisp, percussive quality that can be used to good effect in situations where chords need to be rhythmically articulated. This produces that characteristic stabbing sound that has been so well exploited in trance and other such styles of dance music. You can hear an

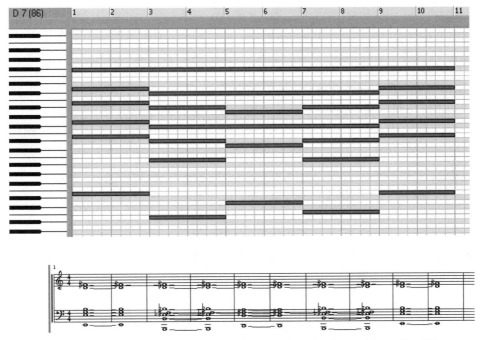

Figure 11.3 Legato strings used as a pad sound (Track 53 on the audio CD).

excellent example of this overdriven type of pizzicato string sound in the main riff of Faithless' "God Is a DJ." That said, you can use pizzicato strings in a great variety of situations. In Figure 11.4, you can see pizzicato strings used in the context of a slower, more relaxed tempo.

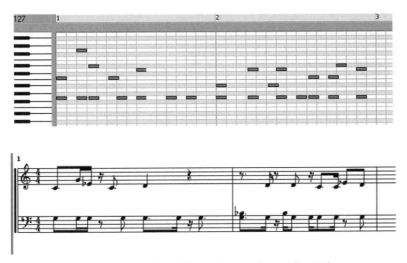

Figure 11.4 Pizzicato strings (Track 54 on the audio CD).

Staccato Strings

Another popular type of bowing is staccato bowing, where the bow is bounced off the string. This produces anything from a light, bouncy string sound to a more aggressive kind of string stab. Staccato bowing is particularly useful when string chords are repeated in a rhythmic fashion. This style of string writing works really well in hip-hop styles and can be used on the quarters, eighths, or a pattern derived from sixteenths. For an example of this kind of string writing, listen to Coldplay's "Viva la Vida."

The example in Figure 11.5 uses staccato bowing with chords on the quarter notes. To emulate staccato bowing, you need to use very short note values.

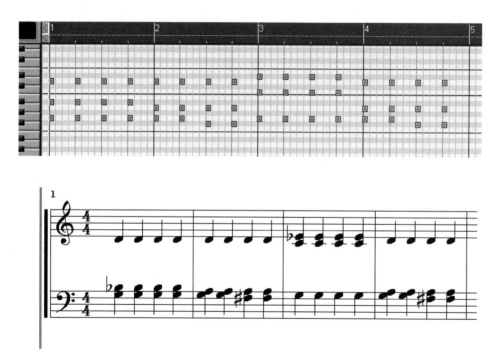

Figure 11.5   Staccato bowing on the quarters (Track 55 on the audio CD).

To write this type of texture, you need to work out the chords that you are going to use first, together with their harmonic rhythm—that is, the points where they change in the phrase. Having worked these out, it is then a simple matter of breaking up the chords into the number of stabs required. Therefore, in the example in Figure 11.5, the first chord of G minor is broken up into four stabs.

Detache Strings

Another important style of string playing is non-legato, also known as *detache*. Here the bow changes direction for each note, producing a lighter, more broken-up tone that is very suitable for faster passages. In an orchestra, strings tend to play all sorts of rapid arpeggios and figuration, which contributes a sense of motion to the music. Just think of Vivaldi's *The Four Seasons*, and you will get what I mean.

You can emulate the detached style of playing using a combination of velocity and notes slightly shorter than the intended note resolution, allowing a minute break between each note. Naturally, the notes of the strongest velocity would tend to be on the strong points of the measure. However, sampled strings are often quite mushy in terms of their attack response. To counteract this, you should set the attack slider of the amplitude envelope to minimum so that each note has an immediate attack.

The most obvious use for non-legato styles of playing is to produce arpeggios. These can be written by evolving a suitable arpeggio pattern for, say, one bar and then copying and pasting it into as many bars as you need. Having done this, then change the relevant notes to follow the harmony. To demonstrate this, I will take the chord progression used in the last example—Figure 11.5—and turn it into a suitable string arpeggio passage (see Figure 11.6).

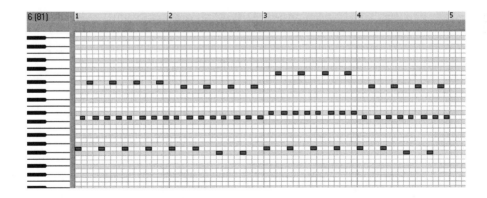

Figure 11.6 String arpeggios emulating non-legato bowing (Track 56 on the audio CD).

Octave Strings

When classical composers want to emphasize a string lead, they will often double it in octaves. This produces a powerful, soaring type of string sound, often called *octave strings*, that works well in certain contexts. Composers of film music often use octave strings for their leads, and it is a type of lead that has come to be associated with the film scores of John Barry, who scored the music for some of the earlier James Bond films. And I am sure, now that I have mentioned James Bond, you know the kind of string lead I am talking about. A more recent example of a famous track that uses octave strings is Kinobe's "Slip Into Something" on the album *Soundphiles*.

Some synthesizers and samplers will have octave string patches on board, but if not, to re-create the sense of octave strings, simply copy your lead and paste it an octave higher. Give it a big, hall reverb and plenty of delay, and you will have that characteristic soaring octave strings lead sound. In Figure 11.7, you can see an example of this type of lead being heard over a string pad chordal background. Unfortunately, I cannot show the staff view because it would be too small to read, covering 15 bars.

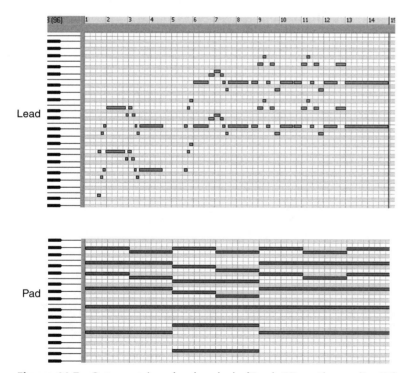

Figure 11.7 Octave strings lead melody (Track 57 on the audio CD).

If you want an even bigger octave strings sound, put the melody and its duplication an octave higher on separate channels, one panned left and the other panned right. Then detune them, say +7 cents for one channel and −7 cents for the other. Then put a tiny delay on one channel.

Tremelo Strings

Tremolo strings are most often used in film music to create an eerie atmosphere or a feeling of tension. In this style of playing, the performer rapidly alternates between two notes to create a quivering sound. Tremolo strings are a fairly popular addition to the spectrum of string patches, so you should have no difficulty obtaining this kind of string sound should you require it.

Conclusion

This chapter has shown that you can use strings in a wide variety of ways and contexts. They can be used effectively as a solo instrument or indeed as one of a number of generic types of string ensemble sound. It has also shown that it is important to know what the real instrument can do and the different ways in which it can be played, because these techniques and styles of playing determine the exact type of string sound obtained, whether that be legato strings, pizzicato strings, staccato strings, tremolo strings, and so on. Bear in mind, though, that this chapter represents no more than a brief survey of some of the generic styles of string playing and that a deeper study of this area will reveal even more about the subject.

12 Writing for Pads

Pads are synthesizer patches that, as their name suggests, are primarily suitable for use on long sustained tones and passages. They can be used either in addition to or in place of legato strings to add warmth, atmosphere, and background ambience to your tracks. The principal value of pads over strings is one of color: Pad sounds can be dark, earthy, light, airy, fluid, ethereal, and so on. Often used at the very background of a track, they can be used as an adjunct to reverb, as a means of setting up a sense of space, atmosphere, and color within the track. Pad sounds are also a very effective way of introducing a track. "Twisted" by Ultra Nate provides a fine example of this type of pad use.

Using Pads

Often with a pad sound, it is enough to play just a single note to set the atmosphere. In Track 58 on the CD, you will hear just a single note being played using Korg's atmospheric Aquaphonics pad patch. I don't know about you, but I find the sound of just this one note to be full of atmosphere and presence (see Figure 12.1).

Within the range of a given pad timbre, by using the synthesizer's on-board controls you can obtain great variations of tone. When automated, these can be used to create continually evolving and transforming soundscapes. Alternatively, they can be used to create pad sounds that rhythmically pulsate. On Track 59 on the CD, you hear Reason's Malstrom pad In Memoriam, in which a series of sustained ninth chords are played. The rhythmic pulsation you hear was obtained by automating the filter frequency A and B (see Figure 12.2).

Pads offer a great alternative to the sound of strings in musical passages that use drones, long sustained tones, and rich ambient chords. Ambient, chill-out, relaxation, and new-age music often tend to be pad-driven, and they are styles of music that take great advantage of the beautiful sensual sound that can be obtained when complex chords such as ninths and elevenths are presented on pads. Tracks 51 and 52 on the audio CD use pads in this particular fashion.

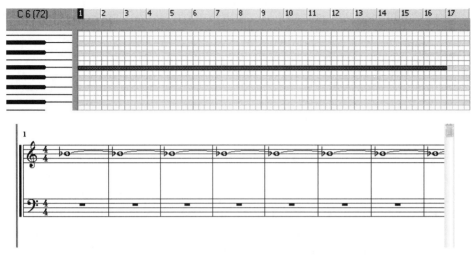

Figure 12.1   Sustained tone on Korg's Aquaphonics pad (Track 58 on the audio CD).

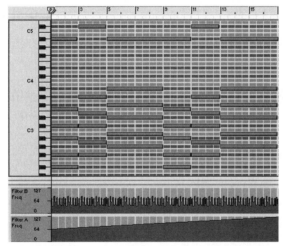

First eight bars:

Figure 12.2   In Memoriam pad with rhythmic pulsation (Track 59 on the audio CD).

Many other styles of music also benefit from the use of pads. Trance and hard dance styles tend to use pads during the breakdown sections—those periods of the track when the drums are taken out and the focus is placed instead on more ambient material. In psy-trance, ambient material is often used in the introductory section. Here the use of pads, along with samples of natural sounds, such as bird songs, is a very common feature. Similarly, in the drum and bass style, ambient material is often used in the dropouts—the two periods in the track where the drums and bass are relaxed in order to give a time of pause before the drums and bass come back in with a new energy and intensity. In fact, no matter what style of music you write, it will always benefit from the use of pads, even if that use is only a very subtle and discreet one.

Types of Pads

You can find the original archetypes of pad sounds in the resources of orchestral music, where for particular expressive purposes composers use passages composed of long sustained tones. The use of legato strings in this context has already been mentioned. But there is also the cooler sound of wind instruments, which offers composers another option. A sustained chord on winds has a cool serenity that is hard to equal. Then there is the warmer, fierier sound of the brass instruments. Horns and trombones together produce a strong and stately type of sustained sound. And of course there is the spectrum of sustained sounds that can be produced by the choir, ranging from the unearthly sound of soft female voices to the more robust sound of the entire choir. When these resources are backed up by tuned percussion instruments, the sense of atmosphere can be greatly enhanced, whether through the rippling arpeggios of the harp, the silvery notes of the celesta, or the bell-like sounds of finger cymbals.

One of the principal strengths of synthesizers lies in their amazing ability to reproduce this wide and diverse range of traditionally sourced orchestral pad sounds. This means that through the use of synthesizer technology, we do not need to have the resources of an entire orchestra to take advantage of them. Yet additionally, many of the pad sounds produced by synths are totally unique timbres that have no parallel whatsoever in the world of live acoustic instruments. And as music producers, we are very fortunate to have this spectrum of resources available to us.

Generally, there are two kinds of pad sounds that you will use—slow synth patches and motion synth patches. The difference between the two is that in the former case the pad timbre tends to be fairly stable, while in the latter case the pad sound is continually modulating. For the ear, this simply means that a motion synth pad will have a continually evolving surface texture. The way in which the synth pad modulates all depends upon the source of the modulation. This can involve the use of filters, low-frequency oscillators, and so on. Sources of modulation of this sort are often intrinsic to the patch concerned. A fine example of the use of motion synth pads in a track is Aril Brikha's "Deeparture in Time."

Pads that use filters for their modulation effects include sweeps, a type of pad sound in which the filter frequency cut-off is gradually raised or lowered. This produces a swooshing type of pad sound that is great for certain types of emphasis. These types of sound are very commonly used in psy-trance. In Figure 12.3, you can see some of the types of pad patches on the ES2 synthesizer in Logic. Their imaginative names aptly suggest their often evocative natures.

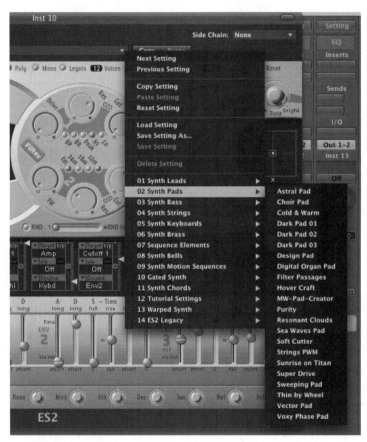

Figure 12.3   Pad patches in Logic Express. The ES2 synth in Logic Express has a nice range of warm pad sounds.

Conclusion

Writing for pads is a relatively straightforward affair because they simply follow the harmony of the music. You have probably heard the term *sound bed*. This refers to the use of subtle background pads upon which the more active layers of the music are written. These are used to add a particular background atmosphere, such as a blue sky on a summer day or a brooding, dark sky as a storm approaches. In Track 51 on the CD, the pad is used to suggest the rising and falling of the ocean waves.

Because many pad effects are quite subtle, do not be afraid to use them in a very discreet way. Even if the volume slider on the pad mixer channel is set very low down, the pad itself will still contribute its own particular color to the mix. It is also well worth experimenting with creating layers of pad sounds that lie upon one another, rather like different layers of sedimentary rock. Such experiments can be used to create beautiful, full, and warm sound textures.

13 Writing for Acoustic Instruments

Some of the most popular sounds used by the computer musician often come from acoustic instruments, such as pianos, saxophones, organs, harps, horns, guitars, and so on, together with various electric equivalents of some of these—electric guitar, electric piano, and so on. Also included in this category are numerous types of ethnic instruments, such as the mandolin, bamboo flute, sitar, pan pipe, shakuhachi flute, zither, tar, and so on.

Challenges with Acoustic Instruments

All of these instruments—and many others not included here—have one powerful feature in common: They are all real, live instruments. Consequently, their use is always going to be problematic for the computer musician. You will often find yourself working alone in your own home studio, and you will not generally have live performers and instruments with which to play your tracks. This means that should you want, say, a Japanese shakuhachi flute part in your music, you will have to write it yourself using what is probably a synthesized emulation or a sample patch of the real instrument.

This automatically presents a number of problems. For a start, it becomes necessary to find decent emulations of those instruments. Here it is notable that the quality of available emulations of acoustic instruments varies greatly, although there are always new plug-ins coming out to help with this matter of quality. Examples of this are LinPlug's SaxLab, a plug-in that offers decent emulations of various types of saxophone, and Band in a Box, which offers some very realistic-sounding guitars. There are also some very good orchestral plug-ins available for those who would like to experiment with some of the more classically oriented instruments.

The Importance of Research

There are so many instruments that belong to this general category that a huge encyclopedia would need to be written to cover and discuss both the instrument and the technique used to play it. Within the space of this short book, the best that I can hope to offer is the sound advice that I have always followed. Whatever plug-ins you use, it is vitally important to study the original instruments themselves. The way in which we looked at strings in Chapter 11 represents a prime example of both the value and the method behind this approach. How do performers actually play the instrument? What is the norm with regard to the playing style(s) for that particular instrument? Are there any particular idiosyncratic techniques often used in association with it?

Before even attempting to write for a particular instrument, it is advisable to try to be able to answer these questions. To do so will probably entail some research and studious listening on your part. As a parallel to this, think of the case of a writer producing a novel set in a particular location during the 18th century. You would expect the writer to do some very precise background research about the history, geography, and layout of the locality in which the novel is set. Without such research there is the serious risk that the entire novel will come across as being totally absurd.

It is exactly the same with writing for an acoustic instrument. A certain amount of background research needs to be done so you can write for it with confidence and in a realistic and authentic way. If you do not do this, the music that you write for a particular instrument is liable to sound amateurish, silly, or even comic. In effect this means that it is not really enough for a track to sound just like, say, a guitar. It must also sound like a guitar would actually be played. In other words, if you are going to write for guitar, spend some time finding out what represents normal technique as far as playing the guitar is concerned.

A simple example of this in the case of the guitar is the strum. If you write a chord for the guitar, and all of the notes sound simultaneously, this would not agree with the way in which a chord is played on the guitar. It is impossible to sound all six strings simultaneously. Consequently, the strings must be strummed, either from the bottom to the top or the top to the bottom. What is the best way to emulate this process of strumming using, say, a MIDI keyboard and a suitable guitar patch? An obvious solution would be to play the notes in as a chord and then manually separate them slightly to emulate a strum. And then there is the technique of picking, in which the notes of the chord are presented as an arpeggio. What is the best way to depict that picking within the limitations of your sample patch? What are the best notes to emphasize? How can they be emphasized?

Remember to try to find out whether there are any specialized types of techniques associated with the playing of that instrument. In the case of the guitar, there is the obvious technique of producing guitar harmonics—those beautiful bell-like sounds that guitarists get by touching the nodes of the string. What is the best way to emulate these, given the limitations of the devices you have available?

This approach needs to be extended to all cases where you use an emulation of an instrument that real performers play:

1. Make sure the sound is realistic, which means you need to get hold of a decent emulation and apply appropriate effects to it (reverb, chorus, and so on).

2. Study the way in which the instrument is played so you can create a decent emulation of that playing technique. Watch out for specialized techniques or features associated with particular instruments, such as pitch bends on the sitar, intonation on Balinese gamelan instruments, harp glissandi, and so on. In Figure 13.1, you can see a particular specialized type of tuning applied to a zither to make it sound it more realistic.

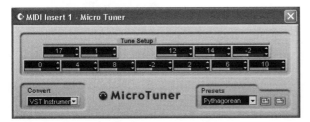

Figure 13.1 Pythagorean tuning applied to a traditional zither makes the sound much more realistic.

Conclusion

This chapter talked about the importance of the use of acoustic instruments in general, together with the difficulties a computer musician might face when trying to both get hold of and use emulations of such instruments within their compositions. It also pointed out that as well as getting hold of decent emulations of the instruments that you want to use, you must research how those instruments are played—and in particular, find out about any characteristic techniques that are particular to those instruments. Here I should point out that although this requires a certain degree of research, any study undertaken in this direction will always prove of great benefit to you. It will enable you to write in a fitting and appropriate way for a given instrument. This, in turn, will lead you to produce much more professional-sounding music tracks.

14 Arpeggiation

For today's modern electronic and popular music, repetition has become one of the major forces in the building up of musical structures. The unit of repetition is generally termed the *loop*, and for many styles of modern music, such as techno, trance, house, and hip-hop, the musical content can often be reduced to a series of simple loops that have been ingeniously combined by the producers to create a complete piece of music.

To be able to compose and produce such music is often a matter of creating a number of suitable loops and then combining them in a satisfactory way within a larger overall structure. Naturally, these loops will have a job to perform within the composition as a whole. There will be drum and percussion loops, bass loops, lead loops, SFX loops, and so on.

What Is an Arpeggiator?

One of the main tools used by computer musicians to generate looped material is the arpeggiator. An arpeggiator itself produces no sound; it is simply a mechanical generator of signals that controls the tempo, pitch, velocity, gate, and other such parameters of the sound produced by a synthesizer or sampler to which the arpeggiator has been routed.

The principal disadvantage of the arpeggiator is that it is a mechanical device, and therefore it can lead to the production of a very mechanical and lifeless sound. Its advantage, however, is that it can produce complex, intricate, and rapid patterns of sound that a live performer would often struggle to be able to play. So I suppose this is a matter of plusses and minuses. What you lose in one area, you gain in another.

Features of an Arpeggiator

The following sections discuss important features to look out for in an arpeggiator.

Monophonic/Polyphonic

A polyphonic arpeggiator has the advantage over a monophonic arpeggiator because it can produce more than one note at the same time. This is great for creating drum patterns, chordal riffs, guitar strumming patterns, and any other pattern you might require. A monophonic arpeggiator, on the other hand, is limited to the production of patterns involving only a single note for each step of the pattern. To overcome this limitation, you can use a monophonic arpeggiator in overdub recording mode, in which one layer of the intended polyphonic pattern is created at a time.

Pitch Control

This provides a way of controlling the pitch of each note produced. Here, there are two levels of control that are desirable. First, there is the fixed pitch mode, where each step of the arpeggio is given a predefined pitch. This is really useful for creating drum patterns using synthesized or sampled drum kits in which each sample has been assigned its own particular key. It is also particularly useful for producing basslines, a process that we discussed in Chapter 7. Second, there is the normal mode, which is a movable pitch arpeggio pattern that will arpeggiate whatever chord is being played on the keyboard. The usefulness of this mode is that the arpeggio will change in accordance with the specific notes being played.

Number of Octaves

This determines the range of octaves the arpeggio pattern will have. A four-octave range will repeat the arpeggio successively over four octaves, and so on.

Note Resolution

This determines the note value of each step, whether an eighth, eighth triplet, sixteenth, sixteenth triplet, thirty-second, and so on.

Gate Control

The gate control is an important parameter because it decides the length of each step relative to the note resolution. Most arpeggiators enable you to specify the gate for the entire pattern. Some of the better arpeggiators, however, let you set the gate individually for each step. This is a really useful ability because it enables you to create a more life-like and rhythmically articulated arpeggio pattern.

Velocity Control

This again is an essential feature because it defines the relative volume of the pattern. Some of the better arpeggiators enable you to set the velocity for each individual note.

This is also a really useful ability because it enables you to create patterns with more dynamic variation and interest.

Tempo Control
This defines the tempo, enabling the arpeggio to sync with the exact speed of the track.

Swing Control
This determines the degree of swing from 0 to 100, with 51 to 100 signifying regular swing and 0 to 49 signifying negative swing (in which the swing is in favor of the second note).

Pattern Control
With arpeggiators you often get a good number of preloaded patterns. Pattern control enables you to select an appropriate pattern, to edit that pattern, and to sequence it as required onto the track.

Curve Control
This enables the arpeggiator to be used to generate control data curves as opposed to pitch patterns. This is great for creating patterns of gating, filtering, and other such modulation patterns, which can bring great interest and variety to a track.

Example of an Arpeggiator
In Figure 14.1 you can see the RPG-8 Monophonic Arpeggiator, which comes with Reason.

Figure 14.1   RPG-8 Monophonic Arpeggiator.

Looking at this device, you can see many of the features that tend to be typical of arpeggiators in general. On the top left you can see a velocity control that sets the velocity levels for the pattern as a whole. Ranging from 1 to 127, this enables arpeggios to be produced within a fairly wide dynamic range. Below the velocity control is an octave range setting, which enables the arpeggio to be placed in any required octave. Toward the center of the device are controls that enable the setting of various pattern options. Using these, you can create any number of generic arpeggio types you might need to use in a composition. These include the standard up, down, down and up, and so on. At the bottom center, you can see the gate control, while the right is an interesting feature that enables you to include rests in the arpeggio pattern. This allows you to create patterns with a greater degree of rhythmic definition.

The notes this arpeggiator plays are determined by the notes played on the MIDI keyboard. If a chord of C minor is played, the arpeggiator will arpeggiate this chord within the terms of the settings you have created for it on the arpeggiating device. In this way, you can play a chord progression, and the arpeggiator will precisely follow that progression.

Uses of Arpeggiators

The full uses of arpeggiators are limited only by your imagination. They can be used to fulfill many tasks. The last chapter spoke about writing for acoustic instruments. Arpeggiators can be used to create idiomatic styles of writing characteristic of particular instruments. In Figure 14.2, you can see an example in which an arpeggiator has been used to create a harp accompaniment to a string passage. You can hear this on Track 60 on the audio CD, and although the arpeggio is a very simple one, it provides a very effective and atmospheric way of bringing a sense of motion to the otherwise static string chord texture.

Figure 14.2 Strings and harp arpeggio—first eight bars (Track 60 on the audio CD).

Unfortunately, it is not practical to provide the piano roll view, because the juxtaposition of the different tracks makes it impossible to compress into a viable graphic.

You can put arpeggiators to good use triggering samples. In the example in Figure 14.3, a single chord sample is being played by an arpeggiator, which generates the chordal pattern and its repetition an octave higher each time. This represents an example of a two-octave range arpeggio.

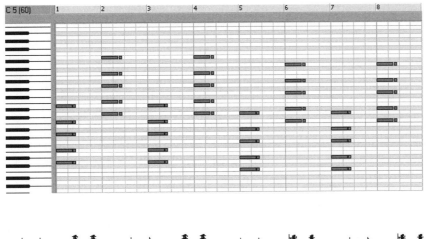

Figure 14.3 Arpeggiator applied to chordal stab (Track 61 on the audio CD).

In virtually every single style of electronic music, arpeggiators are used to generate active layers of music. These layers can be used in any register required, and their use helps to push the music forward and give it a sense of motion and impetus. Figure 14.4

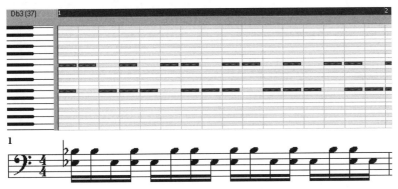

Figure 14.4 Active layer arpeggio (Track 62 on the audio CD).

shows an example of a simple one-bar arpeggio pattern that does just that. The changes in tone that you can hear result from the automation of the filter frequency.

Notice that this is an eight-step pattern and that it would therefore synchronize with a 4/4 beat. Other alternatives are five-, seven-, nine-, and eleven-step patterns, which, being offset from the beat, create interesting pattern variations.

Writing Riffs

A *riff* is any strong and readily identifiable melodic pattern sequence. Riffs are used in many styles of electronic music, particularly trance, techno, and house music. Repeated through the course of a track, they help to establish the character and identity of the music, as well as provide a sense of unity and cohesion. Arpeggiators can of course be used to produce riffs. However, if you want a greater degree of control and artistic creativity, now that you understand what an arpeggiator does, you can write your own arpeggio patterns straight onto the sequencer track using a pencil tool.

When writing a riff, the most important feature to establish first are the melodic guide tones, which will give the riff its melodic shape and character. They are called *guide tones* because they are the melodic notes that the listener tends to pick out from the overall arpeggio pattern, as opposed to the harmonic notes that provide the chordal fill. To demonstrate this, we will go through an example of writing a riff using a step-by-step approach.

Say, for example, that you want to create a one-bar riff in the key of E minor. The first job, as stated above, is to establish the melodic guide tones. These offer the framework around which the riff can be built, and they ensure that it has a tuneful and melodic shape—one that the listener can easily enjoy and appreciate. In Figure 14.5, the initial melodic guide tones have been written in so you can see them. Notice that the line simply rises up through Notes E, G, A, and B (key of E minor). A rising line of this sort tends to give an impression of increasing energy and excitement, so it always represents a good option for the creation of riff material.

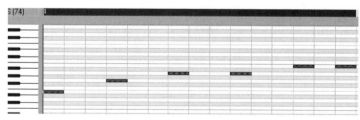

Figure 14.5 Riff melodic guide tones.

After you have written in the guide tones, the next job is to decide the harmonic background of the riff. Being in the key of E minor, the tonic chord of E minor readily suggests itself. This chord will determine which notes will be sounded in the arpeggio. These are then placed at the appropriate points. One such solution would be what you see in Figure 14.6.

Figure 14.6 Addition to the riff of E minor arpeggio tones.

Notice that the arpeggio notes that have been placed all belong to the prevailing E minor harmony—namely the Note E, which is the root, and the Note B, which is the fifth of the chord. These arpeggio notes fill in most of the sixteenths not taken up by the guide tones. This gives the arpeggio that rapid sense of motion required of the riff. The occasional gap also tends to give the riff more rhythmic clarity. When the harmony of a riff needs to be changed, it is a simple matter of changing either the melodic guide tones and/or the arpeggiated notes in accordance with the new harmony. You can hear this in Track 63 of the audio CD. The riff is played for eight bars, and then it changes chord from E minor to A minor for a further four bars before returning to the original tonic chord.

This particular technique is not only useful for trancelike riffs, but it can also be used in any style of music where a riff is required.

Conclusion

If you want more information on arpeggiation, there is a whole chapter on the subject in my book *Music Theory for Computer Musicians* (Course Technology PTR, 2008). Discovering more about the subject is also a matter of gaining experience in the use of arpeggiators and applying them to the solution of musical problems. You can gain this experience through endless experimentation with your arpeggiator—experimentation that explores all of the possible parameters available to you. Through this, you will gain a clear idea of what arpeggiators are capable of and how they are capable of contributing to the creation of music tracks within your particular style.

15 Sampling

A *sample* is usually understood to be an excerpt that has either been *ripped* or *copied* from the recording of another artist or artists. This excerpt is then used in a new, original work, which often bears little or no resemblance to the work from which the original sample was taken. A notable example of this is the use of excerpts from Samuel Barber's "Adagio for Strings" in numerous trance tracks. Comparing the work from which the sample was taken with the work in which the sample is used, it is obvious that they could not be any more different. The former is a classical work written for string orchestra, while the latter are essentially electronic works written in a more modern dance style. It is this often fundamental difference between the two that dispels the idea that the use of samples is tantamount to unoriginality at best and simple theft at worst. Indeed, the composition in which the sample is used is often marked by a high degree of originality in its own right.

Many of the earliest hip-hop tracks made great use of sampling. Rather than using drum machines, sampled breaks were used to produce the percussion. The "Amen Break" produced by the Winston Brothers in the '60s represents the most famous example of this.

The Morality of Sampling

In essence, sampling represents the continuance of a practice that goes back more than a thousand years. Throughout this period, composers have taken freely from other musical works. And despite what anybody might say, this is not usually for the purposes of theft, but because the taken content has inspired the composer's creativity to create a completely new work. Just look at Vaughan Williams' *Fantasia on a Theme by Thomas Tallis*. This beautiful classical work stands entirely on its own merits, despite the fact that it was inspired by and uses a theme written by another composer. Sampling in this respect is something quite healthy, especially for the vitality and vibrancy of the language of music as a whole, because it enables the creation of new types of music through the cross-fertilization of musical ideas. And composers unanimously tend to support this process.

Where the moralities of sampling do start to get a bit hazy is when the user does not acknowledge the sample, because this deliberate lack of acknowledgement carries with it the intimation that the user is trying to claim the idea as his own. Yet in reality, this might not be the user's intention. He or she might simply be trying to avoid the costs of using a sample or the hassle of getting it cleared for use, a process which will be discussed at the end of this chapter.

Another hazy area is where the sample(s) represent the most substantial parts of the music track. 2 Live Crew's "Pretty Woman" (1989), which used drums, bass, and guitar from Roy Orbison's original song of the same name, is a good example, although it might be argued that this song was a parody of the original and therefore represented an example of fair use—that is, the use of copyrighted material for the purposes of education or criticism.

Ripping Samples

There are numerous effective ways to rip samples. One way is to import the track from which the sample is to be taken as an audio file within a DAW, such as Cubase, SONAR, or Logic Express. Once imported in this way, the required sample can then be cut and saved as a WAV or AIFF file within a sample folder set aside for this purpose. The given sample is then freely available for use either on a separate audio track or within a software sampler. The sample can also be time-stretched if necessary—that is, its length can be altered to suit the tempo of the music without any raising or lowering of the pitch.

Another option is to open up the track within an especially dedicated audio editor program, such as Sony Creative Software's Sound Forge (see Figure 15.1). The sample is then cut and pasted as a new file, which is then saved in a sample folder in whatever format suits the user. The processing power of such programs is often significant, which means that the sample can then be EQ'd if necessary, reversed, or modified through the use of audio effects and then normalized to whatever level is needed. However, I would recommend that when you *do* cut samples, you refrain from applying effects until the sample has been imported into your composition. This way, you can treat the sample much more freely, as raw material rather than as already processed material.

1.   Open up the track within Sound Forge.

2.   Zoom in and select the area to be sampled and copy it.

3.   Paste the sample into a new document and save as a WAV file.

4.   Import the sample into a suitable sampler.

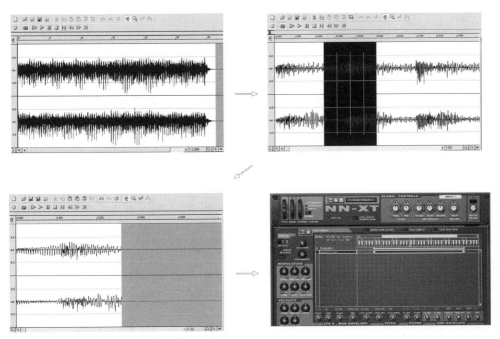

Figure 15.1 Ripping a sample using Sony Creative Software's Sound Forge.

Propellerhead produces a program called ReCycle for the purposes of ripping samples and audio editing in general. ReCycle can automatically chop the sample up into contiguous slices and then save it as a Dr.Rex2 file (see Figure 15.2). This facility is great for sampling drums because it allows you to isolate individual drum shots and use them on their own. It is also great for vocal samples because you can isolate individual syllables, sounds, or words and use them as separate samples in their own right. Those willing to experiment can also find many other great uses.

1. Open the track in ReCycle.

2. Zoom in and set the left and right locators to the required beginning and ending of the sample. Perform the crop loop operation so that only the sample is left. Normalize it to obtain the optimum level for the sample, if required.

3. Using the sensitivity slider, divide the sample up into however many slices you need. The program automatically detects suitable points for the creation of slices, although you can also set these manually.

4. Save the resultant sample as a Dr.Rex file. Open it using a Dr.Rex device and sequence the sample into your track wherever needed. You can treat each slice

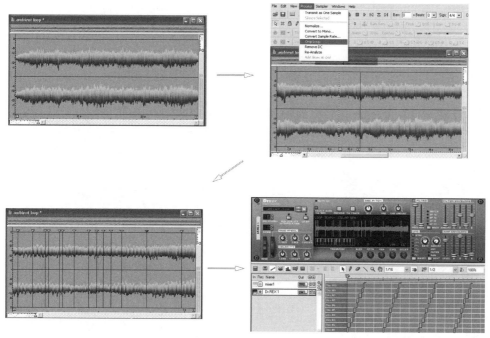

Figure 15.2 Ripping a sample and converting it into a Dr.Rex2 file.

as an individual sound and insert it wherever you want it. You can also import individual Dr.Rex slices into channels of the Redrum machine and use them as individual drum hits, if required.

Developing Your Own Sample Library

Any type of sound that has been recorded falls under the general remit of today's sampling and sampling practice. The speeches of Martin Luther King are a popular sample source, as are excerpts of speech from movies and TV programs. Natural sounds are also commonly used sample sources: the sounds of rain, thunder, birdsongs, flowing water, the slamming of a door. On the Internet you can find many copyright-free sample sources. These can include hits from old drum machines, samples of real drums, *a cappella* vocals, orchestral hits, and so on. You can also freely obtain CDs of samples of all possible types. Do you know of a local market where somebody sells old CDs, cassette tapes, and vinyl? Then get down there and buy up everything you can. Such old recordings can provide a veritable wealth of sample material.

Through the deliberate collection of samples, you will gradually build up your own extensive sample library. The more samples you have in your library the better, because you never know when you might desperately need a particular sample. Imagine this: You can see the scene you want to portray in the introduction to your track—a steamy tropical rainforest full of the songs of exotic birds. To your sample library you go, and because you have been diligently collecting samples, there are numerous options available to you. From there it is just a matter of loading the sample, and off you go. If you didn't have those samples on hand, you would have to hunt them down, a process that could possibly interrupt the creative flow of musical ideas. Suffice it to say, the more extensive your sample library, the greater the creative freedom you will enjoy.

Creating Your Own Sample Patches

As you build your sample library, you will also start to build up and create your own sample patches—that is, patches composed of multi-samples mapped across the keyboard. Sample patches are absolutely brilliant because you can load maybe a hundred different samples into a single patch. Sample patches are also a good way to organize your sample library. Need a reverse cymbal sound for a particular situation? Simple, just load your Reverse Cymbal 1 sample patch, and away you go. Need the sound of flowing water in your track? Again, simple—just load the sample patch Sounds of Water.

Creating sample patches takes time and effort, but it can be fun as well. How you create them and in what format depends upon your setup. While hardware samplers, such as the Akai series, have held the market for a long time now, the quality and capability of software samplers, such as those produced by HALion for example, have so improved that they are now viable (if not equally good) alternatives to a hardware sampler. Most DAWs also offer their own onboard samplers, such as the EXS-24, which comes with Logic Express. Which sampler(s) you use all comes down to your personal setup and preferences. I really appreciate the qualities of the Reason NN-XT Advanced Sampler for the general purpose of creating sample patches (see Figure 15.3). This is a great software sampler, although as you will appreciate, most samplers work along similar lines.

Figure 15.3 The Reason NN-XT Advanced Sampler.

The most important features to grasp when creating your own sample patch are mapping, key zones, and root keys. To create a sample patch, you must load a sample into the sampler and assign it a key or keys. This is called *mapping*. Whether a single key or numerous keys are assigned to a sample depends upon the type of sample and whether you want to use it at numerous pitches. The delicate bell-like sounds of finger cymbals, for example, would benefit from a full chromatic range of sounds so that you could use them in any key required.

When the remote editor of the NN-XT is activated, the instrument unfolds to show you the full extent of its capability (see Figure 15.4).

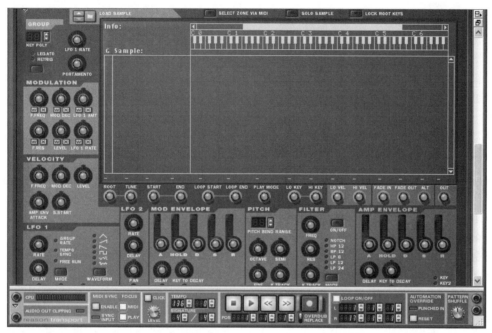

Figure 15.4   NN-XT Remote Editor.

A sample is loaded using the Load Sample tab at the top left. When the sample is selected, it is imported using a default root key C3. This means that when the key C3 is pressed, the sample will be triggered at its actual pitch. If the note D♭ above it is then pressed, the sample will be triggered a semitone higher, and so on. In Figure 15.5 you will see that a kick has been loaded, the intention being to create a sampler patch for a dance drum kit. Below the keyboard you can see the default key zone assigned to each sample, which is quite a large one, covering five octaves.

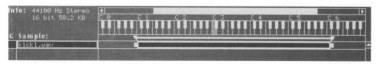

Figure 15.5   Loading a sample.

If you are creating a sampler patch of, say, a hundred different samples, you would use the root key control to bring down the root key to the lowest possible note. Having done this, you would then create the key zone—the range of pitches required to trigger the sample. In this case only one pitch is required, so both of these adjustments are made (see Figure 15.6).

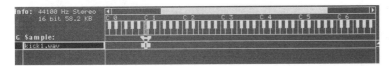

Figure 15.6   Modifying the root key and key zone.

Note that the root key has been lowered to C1 and the key zone has been adjusted to one key. So whenever the key C1 is pressed, it will trigger this particular kick drum sample. The next stage is to load another sample. So the first sample is deselected, and another sample is loaded via the Load Sample tab. In this case it is another kick drum sample. When this has been loaded, the root key is set to D♭1, and the key zone is again set to one key (see Figure 15.7).

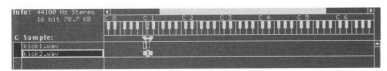

Figure 15.7   Loading another sample.

This process is then repeated until the entire sample patch has been built up. Once you have loaded all of the samples, the patch is then saved with an appropriate name and is ready for immediate use in any of your compositions. In this way, you can build up patches of related samples and store them for future use.

The process has been somewhat simplified for the purposes of explanation. Realistically, you can make many adjustments to each sample once it has been imported. Just look at the great number of controls on the remote editor! These can be applied to every single sample sound. Also, it is possible to assign different outputs to particular samples, thus routing each sample to particular insert effects. The kicks are routed to a compressor, the snare to a reverb device, and so on. These effects, along with the sampler patch, can then also be saved as a Combinator.

It is also possible to apply more than one sample to each key. When these samples are assigned exclusive velocity zones, the velocity of the note will determine which sample will sound. If Sample 1 is set to a velocity zone of 1 to 60, while Sample 2 has a velocity zone of 61 to 127, then with a velocity of 80 you will hear the second sample, while a velocity of 50 will trigger the first. This is really good for drum kits because it can reflect the tonal changes that occur when the same drum is hit at different intensities.

Another approach is to create split-key patches, assigning half of the keyboard to, say, piano and the other half to strings. You can also use both within the same key range, so a note on the piano will also trigger a note on the strings, and so on.

Using a decent sampler, you can see that it is possible to really increase the capabilities of your setup. Need a decent tubular bells patch? Well, get hold of some suitable samples and make your own. In this way, you can build up entire orchestral collections, collections of ethnic and folk instruments, and so on. If you are ever feeling uninspired but don't want to remain musically inactive, spend some time creating sampler patches of your own. Doing this will probably get your musical imagination going, and you will find yourself writing again. Suffice it to say that no time ever needs to be wasted, even if you are going through an unproductive spell.

Resampling

Resampling is a great trick used to increase the capabilities of your setup. To resample, you simply export a track as an audio file and then import it back in again as a sample. In this way, hardly any of the computer's precious CPU is used. Want to create a huge, fat pad sound? Set up a vast number of devices all with applied effects and lay down the music you require. The number of devices involved will probably make great demands on your computer's processing power. However, once you have written your fat pad loop, you simply export it as an audio file and bring it back in again by assigning it to one key of a sampler.

Want to create a vast tribal-drum sound? Again, resampling is the answer. Build up as many layers of complex percussion as you want, and when you have finished, simply resample the whole lot. This frees up your resources to add other elements to the track without fear of overburdening the computer's processing power. In this way you can build up complex layers of sound that ordinarily would bring your computer to a crash point. Assigning each layer to a particular key on your sampler means that you are also free to experiment with layer combinations, with each layer being triggered by a single key. One key you could assign to the drums, another to the bassline, another to the lead, and so on.

As a simple example of resampling, listen to Track 63 on the audio CD. The filtered pad you hear was created by layering a complex chord using strings and pads. It was then resampled and triggered at different pitches, and then I added samples of harp and filtered drums. Although involving the process of resampling, all of the material in this example is nevertheless the author's own original material!

The Legalities of Sampling

I am a firm believer in the use of samples to create new and original works. Many samples, after all, are taken from old recordings that might otherwise lie in obscurity. Sometimes when these are used, a renewed interest in the original recording results. Indeed, it may even become a hit track for a while. This happened when P.M. Dawn took samples from Spandau Ballet's "True" in their record "Set Adrift on a Memory Bliss." Spandau Ballet took the opportunity to re-release their record, and it became an instant hit.

Where samples are being ripped from recordings, there is the complex issue of copyright law to negotiate one's way around. Today's record contracts nearly always contain a clause that stipulates any samples used must be cleared beforehand. Necessarily, this clause protects the record company from being liable to any claims made against them for uncleared samples.

To clear a sample, you must obtain two vital permissions. First, you must obtain the permission of the phonographic copyright holder—that is, the owner of the copyright of the original master recording. This is usually the record company. Second, you must obtain permission from the intellectual copyright holder—that is, the person(s) who own the copyright on the material itself. Without these permissions, you can find yourself involved in a very expensive lawsuit in which up to 100 percent of the royalties obtained from the sale of the track might be given to the original copyright holders.

There is a common belief that the amount of material that is sampled has a bearing, but today this is just not true. You can be sued for any uncleared sample, no matter how small it is—even a tiny snippet of flute melody or a single kick drum sound. Naturally, the degree of interest in an uncleared sample depends largely on how much money the track is liable to make. If the track becomes a hit and there are large royalties at stake, then the lawyers suddenly start to come out of the woodwork. So my advice to you is to be very, very careful and either clear your samples first or don't bother to use them at all. You might also care to look at MACOS—Musicians Against the Copyrighting of Samples—because they produce recordings from which any person is free to use samples provided they extend to any other person the same right with regard to their own track that uses the sample.

Conclusion

The possibilities of sampling are endless, and discussing just the use of samples in the history of modern music would itself fill an encyclopedia. I am sure that the process of sampling will continue, both legally and illegally. Regardless of whether you are interested in ripping samples, the sampler itself represents a valuable music production tool. Knowledgeable use of it will greatly increase your ability to produce professional-sounding recordings.

16 Control Data

A lot of today's music is loop based, which means that it relies mainly on the use of repetition. The unit of repetition is called a *loop*. Whether these loops are drum patterns, bass patterns, riffs, lead material, or pad sounds, the composition of a track will often consist of many of these loops combined together in an interesting and effective way. Yet used in a mechanical and unthinking way, loop-based repetition in music can lead to a quick loss of interest from the listener. Indeed, "the music just does not develop" is a common criticism that could be levied against loop-based productions. Although on the surface this might seem to be true, further examination will often show that it is not. The music does indeed develop, often in many subtle ways, and to appreciate them you must listen to the music in a different way.

When using repetitive, loop-based material, you must give the listener a different focus than the conventional memory and anticipation responses that they are used to when listening to more thematically oriented music. An example of the latter is simple song format in which the chorus section offers a thematic contrast to the verse—a contrast that will often involve a change of both key and mood. This format will be more fully discussed in Chapter 17, "Approaching Structure." For now, just notice that to listen to a piece of music written within this particular format involves both memory and anticipation. Memory is involved in the recognition of the content of the verse and chorus sections. Anticipation is involved where the listener is then led to expect a return of verse or chorus sections. Whether that expectation is fulfilled or frustrated is all part and parcel of the enjoyment of listening to a song. For example, instead of the expected verse, perhaps the songwriter introduces a really interesting solo instrumental section.

Because of this juxtaposition of different types of material, the song itself has a semblance of development; it is offering a musical journey through different territories and keys and thus has a sense of forward progression, a sense of going somewhere. Loop-based music, however, often remains in the same key and involves the continual repetition of discrete musical elements. In effect, this means that the composer must employ different methods of maintaining the listener's interest in the music—methods that do not necessarily depend upon thematic contrast or transformation. It also means that the listener must learn to hear this music in a different way. Rather than listening for thematic contrasts and variations, the listener is instead led to focus on subtle changes that occur within the loops themselves. The interest of the music, in other words, lies in the fact that the listener gradually becomes aware that there is a process of change going on within the repetition of the looped material. This process will involve the use of gradual transformations effected to particular parameters of the loops being used. An example of such changes is the application of filtering effects to a drum track. The drum loop might remain the same in all other respects. Yet by applying a pattern of filtering effects to it, the drum loop acquires a new dimension of interest for the listener.

Changes of Control Data as Process

These days, one of the most powerful means for setting up a process within looped material is through the use of control data. Look at any synthesizer or sampler, and you will see a whole series of knobs, dials, and sliders, each of which controls a particular parameter of the output of that device. Naturally, any change in the settings of these controls will lead to an audible change in the output of that device. When these changes are effected with deliberate intent over a period of time within a composition, this is called a *control data process*. In Figure 16.1, you can see the freeware Superwave synth plug-in.

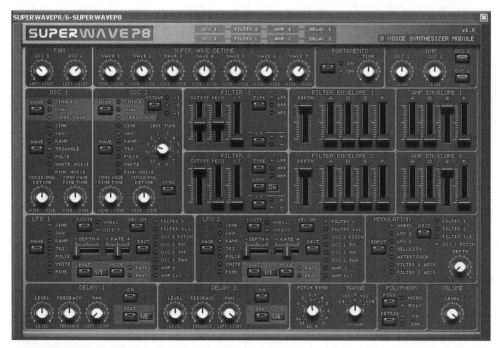

Figure 16.1 Superwave synth.

There is certainly no shortage of controls on this device, every one of which can be used to set up a control data process—that is, a transformation of control data that brings increased interest to the use of looped material. There are the filters, the low-frequency oscillators, panning controls, delay effects, and so on, all of which can prove to be useful tools for the creation of control data processes.

The record of these controls is called *control data*. Changes effected to these controls during the course of a composition can be recorded onto controller lanes, which means that these changes can then become an integral feature of the composition itself. You can also automate these changes using a pencil tool within a given controller lane. In this way, you can set up patterns of control data processes, such as rhythmic panning effects, vibrato effects, or that LFO wobble so popular in drum and bass.

Using these controller lanes can at first seem to be quite daunting, because there is an individual lane available for every parameter. Figure 16.2 shows you just a few of the controller lanes used to affect the output of the Reason Thor synth.

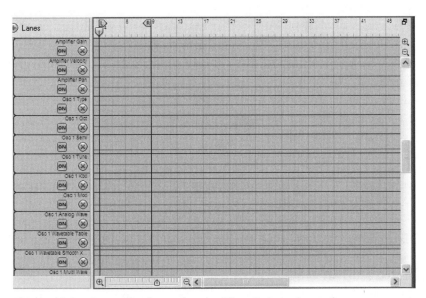

Figure 16.2 Controller lanes for the Thor Polysonic synth.

The most commonsense approach is to set the loop to play and then experiment with the controls and listen to the way in which they affect the sound. If you find something you like, simply record those changes. Then, if you wish to edit them afterward, there will be a controller lane available for that purpose.

Through the use of such control data changes, the looped material will acquire an additional interest to listeners because they will gradually become aware that there is a process of transformation going on within the looped material. The type of transformation will all depend upon the nature of the controller that is being modified. This can involve any controller, belonging both to the synth or sampler and to any effects devices used to process their output.

One of the most common types of control data process applied to looped material is changes made to the filter frequency cut-off. There is something uniquely interesting about this type of process, as a loop comes in at first with the filter frequency cut-off set to the lowest setting. Then, as the filter frequency control is gradually raised, more and more of the high-frequency content starts to come through, leading to a gradual brightening and clearer definition of the sound. Track 64 on the CD provides a clear example of this, in which a rise of filter frequency has been effected over a period of 32 bars.

Another extremely popular type of control change that perhaps everyone can appreciate is the use of the pitch wheel. Virtually every sound-producing device will have a pitch wheel that, when moved, will subtly adjust the pitch of the note being produced by the synthesizer. When moved upward, it causes the raising of the pitch, whereas when moved downward, it causes the pitch to lower. Such subtle changes are often a feature of acoustic instrumental performances, in which perhaps a guitarist introduces a slight pitch bend to a particular note. This gives the performance a greater sense of personal expression. Through use of the pitch wheel on your synthesizer, you can also introduce such expressive changes of pitch. In this respect, even very slight and subtle changes can have the desired effect.

To take advantage of a control data process, it is useful to have a decent MIDI keyboard—one that will allow you to freely assign the controls of your keyboard to particular controller lanes on your sequencer. This gives you the great advantage of being able to experiment and play around with these parameters in real time in order to get an idea of the degree and type of transformation of control data you would like to use. The Korg Control 49 keyboard is a good example of this type of device. Another option is a controller such as the Kaoss Pad, also manufactured by Korg, which allows control data to be manipulated through exerting pressure and directional movement on a touch-sensitive pad. When recorded, this data can also become an integral feature of the final composition.

Another type of control data process is obtained by attaching insert FX to the sound-producing device. A good example of this is a flange effect. Applied in various ways to, say, the drum track, the flange device can introduce some really interesting changes in sound texture—provided, of course, that it is not overdone. Often all that might be required is enabling the device for a couple of bars. This can introduce a sudden change of texture, which can offer a refreshing alternative to the otherwise static sound of the drum track. For more information on this topic, refer to Chapter 10.

Conclusion

In today's electronic music, control data processes can prove to be so important to the music that they can be considered essential tools for the composition and crafting of musical material. You will often find that an intuitive approach to these processes works well. By intuitive, I mean freely experimenting with the onboard synthesizer controls to see how they can be used to shape and affect your material. Once you find something suitable, you can then record and edit it and thereby integrate it into the composition as one of its important features.

Yet whatever control data processes you do introduce into a track, it is important that they be viewed within the perspective of the composition as a whole. Where is the particular passage in which a given process is being used actually heading? Control data processes can often involve gradual transformations over a significant number of bars of the music. The effect of these can be to enhance a build-up or to cause a release of tension. For this reason, control data processes often play a significant part in the structuring of the music—its build-ups, peaks, ebbs, and flows. This brings us on to the next important topic of this book: musical structure.

17 Approaching Structure

A clear understanding of structure is a vital prerequisite to the successful composition of a music track. This is because structure concerns the way in which your musical material is organized and presented in time. Viewing any piece of music as a whole, it is fairly obvious that the whole itself is composed of many parts. Each of these parts is called a *section*, and the piece as a whole is composed of many such sections. Each section, in turn, is made up of numerous other smaller structural parts, such as musical themes and phrases. All of these considered together represent the structure of the music.

Musical Form

Another term for structure is *form*, and where the term *form* is used, it usually refers to a particular type of structure, such as song form (see the upcoming "Song Form" section) or classical sonata form. A historical study of musical form shows that there are a great number of separate forms that have been used and recognized in the history of music. Binary form, ternary form, rondo form, concerto form, variation form, fugal form, aria form, and so on.... For scholars, the study and classification of these is an important concern. However, as music composers, our major concern is the best way to structure our own musical tracks. To do so, you must understand the simple principles that underlie musical forms.

Continuity and Contrast; Repetition and Change

In nearly all cases you will find that the structure or form of music is a result of the application and use of two fundamental principles: *Continuity*, which manifests through processes of musical repetition, and *contrast*, which manifests through processes of musical change. When you view these principles as extremes, it becomes very clear how one needs the other in order to create a balanced whole.

Imagine a piece of music that never repeats anything, where everything is constantly changing. As soon as you hear one theme, off the track goes into another, and then another, and another, and so on. After a while, you will lose interest in this music simply because you will not know, care about, or recognize what you are listening to. The track would come across like insane ramblings on no subject in particular. And then imagine the other extreme: a piece of music where nothing ever changes, where the same idea is exactly repeated over and over again. Once you realized that after the first few bars nothing was ever going to happen in this piece of music, you would soon lose interest in it.

By considering these two extremes, it becomes obvious that the feature that keeps our interest going in a piece of music is the existence of a successful balance and juxtaposition of the familiar element of repetition and the unfamiliar element of change. Musical form or structure is the way in which you achieve this successful juxtaposition.

Song Form

A typical example of a successful juxtaposition of continuity and contrast is the basic form used by most popular songs, a form composed of the two main structurally contrasting elements of the verse and the chorus. After the usual introduction, popular songs tend to go into the first verse. After the first verse you will then often get the second verse. This imprints the verse section firmly in your mind. Were you to bring in another verse at this point, you would risk losing your listeners' interest. Two repetitions are sufficient to imprint the verse section into our memory. So at this point a change occurs—the first chorus comes in, a section that contrasts with the verse not only in terms of the overall mood, but also in terms of its key.

Having set up this interesting contrast between verse and chorus, the third verse then comes in. This represents a return to familiar ground. This return then sets up the listener's anticipation of the return of the chorus. So to the enjoyment of the listener, the chorus comes back. However, having set up this pattern and repeated it, there is now the risk that carrying on repeating it indefinitely would cause the listener to lose interest. So at this point the break often occurs—some new material that you haven't heard before. This refreshes the listener's interest in the song, enabling a further return of the already familiar verse and chorus.

Figure 17.1 shows a summary of this simple but universally effective structure.

In reality you will find many variations and permutations of this basic structure. This is because there are no rigid formulas that offer tried-and-true guarantees of success in terms of musical structure. It all comes down to finding a successful way to balance the familiar with the unfamiliar, repetition and change, continuity and contrast. As long as a musical structure does this, it will be successful.

Yet structure is always a problem within any extended composition. This is because the way in which the music is structured can determine whether the track maintains the listener's interest. For this reason, structure always needs very careful consideration.

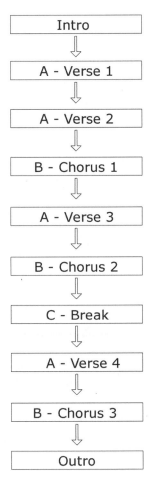

Figure 17.1 Basic song structure.

This especially applies to music that is not essentially lyric-driven. When it comes to a song, the structure will be determined largely by the lyric itself, the music being simply a backing track for the vocalist. In this case, therefore, the writer has something substantial around which to structure the song. Without a lyric, though, the composer is forced to find a workable structure within the musical material itself. Here it is a matter of finding equivalent contrasting elements with which to build the structure, whether these be solo and group, percussive and ambient, or, in the case of dance music, the breakdown and the drop.

Structure in Dance Music

With dance music, the structural elements are largely determined by the purpose of the music itself: to make people want to dance. There is also an additional factor arising from the way in which the music is played—it is mixed by a DJ. For this reason, most dance tracks tend to have drum-led intros and outros—often as much as about 45 seconds or so—called *mix zones*, which give the DJ the opportunity to mix the track in and out. And during the intro, a decent kick-drum beat is helpful for the DJ in the process of beat-matching. Curiously, psy-trance is characterized by ambient intros, but this is a feature that arose in the early days of Goa when, due to the heat, tracks were mixed using cassette decks. Although CD decks are commonly used now, the retention of the ambient intro seems to be more a matter of tradition than of structural necessity.

The existence of a mix zone encourages the earlier phases of dance tracks to involve a buildup of elements: first, perhaps, the drums gradually build up and then after a fashion, maybe the bass is introduced. Then, gradually, other elements are added in, leading up to a peak. There is no formula that specifies the order in which these elements are introduced. As long as there is a definite sense of build, the order itself is irrelevant.

After the initial build, there often comes a breakdown, where the drums tend to be less prominent or even disappear all together to make room for more ambient material. This is a common place for the use of SFX, spoken samples, and so on. The length of the breakdown can, of course, vary depending upon the style. Coming out of the break is an exciting moment as the drums come back in again, often together with some main lead material. This is called the *drop*, and depending upon the style and piece of music itself, there is sometimes a further build leading to a second break and subsequent drop. This final drop often represents that anticipated moment of the highest energy, when everything comes back in and people rush back onto the dance floor.

Again, there are many variations of this basic structural blueprint. Therefore, rather than looking for a formula with which to structure dance music, it is more productive to look at the logic and psychology behind the structure. This is illustrated in Figure 17.2, which represents solutions to the same problem as approached through the style of trance and drum and bass, respectively. You will notice that both use the same essential structural features, but in a different way.

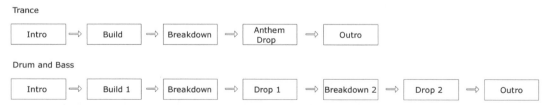

Figure 17.2   Two different solutions to the same problem.

Trance often has some quite epic breakdowns, which can last a considerable amount of time. Therefore, by the time the drop occurs, most of the energy of the track has been fully expended. Drum and bass, on the other hand, is not only much faster and therefore has shorter sections, the breakdowns are often quite short and are written to set up the intense moment of the drop. Within this style, therefore, there is room for two breakdowns and two drops, the second drop being the point where the track peaks.

Study Your Favorite Tracks

The uses of repetition and change are universal principles in structuring all music, no matter what the style. Having grasped this, it is well worth spending some time seeing how these principles apply to your kind of music. This is done through a careful study of successful music tracks belonging to your own particular genre(s). I know of numerous producers who have approached the study of structure in this way. Try it as an exercise. Sit down with pen and paper and listen carefully to one of your favorite music tracks, and note what happens in it and where. By doing this, you will make some very interesting discoveries, because you will find that although much of the music might sound quite spontaneous, it is probably well crafted and very carefully structured.

Observe, for example, the way in which, perhaps, the drums introduce the track over a period of, say, 16 bars. Then the bass comes in and the drums repeat. The lead then comes in at Bar 33, and after a 16-bar lead, the whole thing repeats, but this time without the drums. Then the drums come back in, and the music picks up pace, and so on. Try breaking down a track in this way to see how it is carefully structured. Once you have seen this, you will then have a clear framework that you can apply to your own tracks.

Less Is More

Having seen the necessity for the creation of a good working balance between repetition and change, there is also the matter of the amount of material that a track uses. There is a common saying in music production that less is more. If you study some of the best music tracks, you will discover that the amount of musical material used is often quite minimal. The reason for this is that it is always far more effective to do more with less than less with more. One of the common mistakes would-be producers make when they start out is producing too much material for a track.

Although the material itself might be great, if there is too much of it, the listener literally will feel bombarded by the constant assault of new material. By keeping the amount of material that you use in a track to the bare minimum, you give your listener the room and space to enter into the music, to become absorbed and fascinated by it. The track also comes across as being tight and cohesive in its structure, and it means that there is nothing in the track that is irrelevant or redundant.

The other day I heard "God is a DJ" by Faithless playing on the radio. Listening to this track, I realized that there was hardly any material in it at all. The whole track is built up by alternating two contrasting elements: a simple riff and a voiceover section. Interest in the track is maintained by dropping the drum track in and out and using some uplifting string chords introduced during the breakdown. This represents a perfect example of less being more.

Conclusion

Undoubtedly the most important consideration when structuring your music is to maintain your listeners' interest in it. This is achieved by not using too much repetition or unnecessary changes. The aim is to obtain a perfect balance between these two poles. As you are a listener in your own right, your own ear will often provide the best guide. As soon as your ear starts to tire of the material, it is likely that the listener will experience the same reaction. At this point, therefore, it is time to bring in something new, some contrasting material the listener hasn't heard before. Having done this, you can then make a return to more familiar elements.

Yet before your material is structured into a finished piece, you must lay down that material in the first place. This process is called *layering*. Having layered your material, you can then extend it into that cohesive structure that will mark your track as being a finished product. This process is called *sequencing*. The next chapter will consider these two important processes.

18 Layering and Sequencing

In this chapter we will discuss laying down musical material prior to the process of sequencing, whereby that material is extended into a complete track. We will then consider the process of sequencing itself. The former process is called *layering* because of the particular way in which it is accomplished. Each element, or *layer*, of your music is laid down on a particular channel of your sequencer, with each channel being appropriately labeled and identified.

The type of channel used will depend upon the type of material. Audio material, such as recordings of live instruments and vocals, will be laid down on separate audio tracks. MIDI material will be laid down on the MIDI tracks set aside for this purpose on your chosen sequencer. You can see the separate channels available for this in the Arrange window of Logic Express (see Figure 18.1).

Laying Down the Drum Track

Most producers tend to lay down the drum track first, the principal reason being that it provides a nice, clear beat to work with. It also provides a good way of marking time. Many sequencers have an onboard metronome with which to mark time, although personally, I find these so irritating and intrusive that they actually put me off. Therefore, for me, working to a good drum beat is a much more productive option.

To lay down the drum track, first you must have a very clear idea of what kind of track you are intending to write in terms of its genre, mood, style, and general atmosphere. Most producers tend to have a clear idea of the track in their imagination before they actually write it. This idea could have arrived out of nowhere, triggered by listening to another piece of music, or maybe it was simply inspired by playing around and improvising on the keyboard. Whatever the trigger was, it is helpful if you have a clear vision of the track in your own mind before you start working, because this vision will provide the best guide to your choices as you write the material.

Sometimes the drum beat you use might turn out to be nothing more than a caretaker drum track—that is, a track inserted on one channel that represents a fair approximation

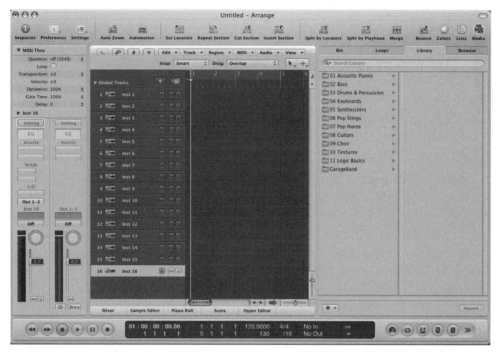

Figure 18.1 Logic Express Arrange window. Logic Express makes it easy to layer your music. You select the channel on the left and an appropriate and suitable instrument for that channel on the right. Then, you are ready to play and record your next layer.

of the type of drums you are going to need. When it comes to layering, however, you must fix that drum track into a clear and concise pattern. Depending upon how many channels your sequencer has, in the long run you will find it more productive to put each separate drum element on its own particular channel. This gives you much greater control over each individual drum sound, as well as setting up really good opportunities for sequencing particular isolated elements of the drum track, such as the hi-hat pattern, for example. When you do this, remember to clearly label each channel. There is nothing worse than looking for the channel on which your cowbells have been laid down amidst what might be 30 or 40 separate unidentified channels.

When each drum sound is on its own channel, it enables you to apply effects individually to each sound, as well as to EQ each individual drum sound to your satisfaction. The level of each sound can also be precisely controlled and monitored. Ideally, you should then send all of your drum channels through to a separate bus (see Figure 18.2). This gives you the additional facility of being able to apply controls and effects to the drum track as a complete whole.

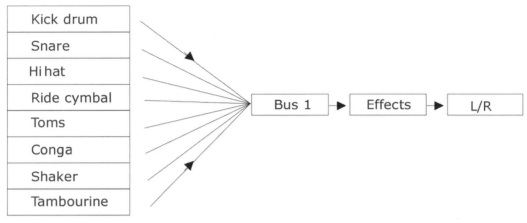

Figure 18.2 Sending drum channels through to an individual bus.

The way in which you do this will all depend upon your setup. Most software mixers offer opportunities for the use of buses. If you're using a program such as Reason, you would set up a dedicated drum mixer to which all of your drum and percussion sounds would be routed (see Figure 18.3). You would then route the output of this mixer to one channel of your main mixer.

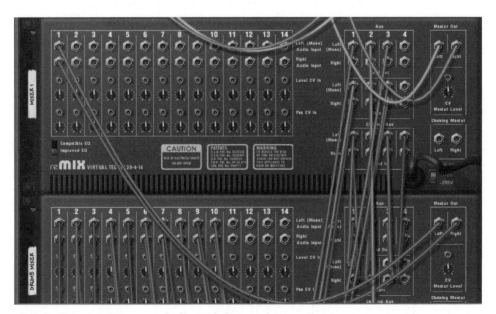

Figure 18.3 Setting up a dedicated drum mixer.

I also know of some producers who like to cable each Redrum channel to a separate drum mixer channel (see Figure 18.4). This gives greater control over each drum sound as well as the opportunity to use the four sends.

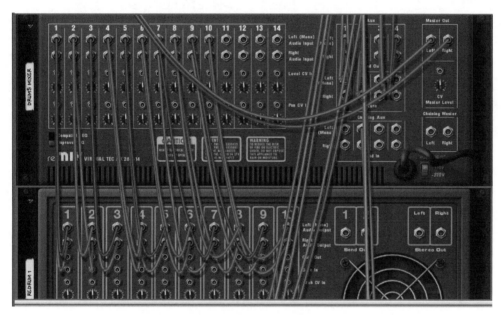

Figure 18.4 Cabling Redrum channels to their own separate mixer channels.

When laying down your drum track, it is vitally important to get the sound just right before you carry on. Every drum sound needs to be clean and clear. Never be lazy and put off problems until the mixing or mastering stage. It is very probable that by then it will be too late anyway. Then you are faced with the horrendous prospect of backtracking to try to eliminate those problems.

It is also a great mistake to try to sequence your track before you have laid down all of the material. There is a high probability that if you do so, you will get stuck at some point. Lay down everything you are going to need beforehand. Once you have done this, you can make sure that everything works together: the bass works with the drums, the lead works with the bass, and so on. And only then should you set about sequencing and extending that material into a whole track. For this reason, all you will initially need in terms of your drum track is a section of, say, eight bars. Having laid this down, set up this section as a loop and begin to lay down your other material.

Laying Down the Bass

Your next priority will probably be to lay down the bassline over the drums you have already laid down. It is wise to start with the bassline, rather than, say, the lead, because the bassline and kick occupy very similar regions of the frequency spectrum. Both also tend to be panned dead center. It is vital to make sure that the bass and kick work together without any conflict and that their respective sounds and frequency placement complement each other well. Primarily, you assess this by ear. Both kick and bass need to be clearly audible, and there should be no undue interference between them. A process of careful listening will provide you with all of this information. Figure 18.5 shows this crucial stage of laying down a bassline within Ableton Live 7.0.

Figure 18.5 Laying down a bassline in Ableton Live.

You also need to listen carefully to the bassline on its own. Ideally, the bassline should be of such a quality that it can stand on its own without the support of any other instrument. If the bassline only sounds good when it is being propped up by something else, then something has gone wrong somewhere. If you do write a bassline of this sort, then you will be greatly restricted later in the piece when you want to bring the drums out but have the bass continue. Without a premium-quality sound all of its own, as soon as the drums drop out, the track will crash. It is therefore very important to write a bassline that sounds great even when soloed.

At this stage, it is wise to make sure that the bassline is heard at its best, without any mud or haze in the sound—that is, unnecessary frequencies that do not serve any real musical purpose. These especially can occur when reverb or delay is applied to the bass. Some basses definitely benefit from these types of effects, but the aim is to get the benefit of the effect with the minimum of hazy interference. If you do get this, try to eliminate it either by drying out the sound some more or by implementing the discrete use of EQ. The clearer and more individual the sound of your bass, the better.

Laying Down Your Lead Material

Once you have your drums and bass working together well, you can think about laying down your lead material. The first issue to approach is the type of lead sound you are looking for. A good lead needs to have a rich, distinctive, and full sound that is going to stand out in the mix. It also needs to work well, in terms of its tonal qualities, with the sound of the bass. Therefore, your first task is to find or create a suitable lead instrument. This could take some time and involve a full exploration of the lead instruments available to you. However, this is all time well spent, because once you have a good lead instrument, its very sound will inspire your creativity.

One such excellent lead is the Juicer II provided as one of the Reason Combinator Patches. As you can see in Figure 18.6, Juicer II makes full use of delay effects, using some six separate delay devices.

The bass and lead together will provide the main elements of the harmony of the music. When these work together effectively, they will provide that necessary underpinning and framework for everything else in the track, whether this will be pad fills, picking on the guitar, chords or keyboard stabs, arpeggio patterns, and so on. Therefore, it is very important for the bass and lead to complement one another and to work together as a unit. For this to occur, they must make complete sense in terms of the harmonic and modal implications of the music you are creating.

When discussing the writing of melodic leads, we considered the importance of both key and mode. Key, you will recall, concerns the tonal center of the music, whereas mode concerns the type of scale used with reference to that tonal center. For bass and lead to work together, you need to consider the issues of both key and mode. What key is the

Figure 18.6 Juicer II—a Reason Combinator Patch.

music in? What mode or scale does it use? What is the chord progression used to guide the bass and lead? The answers to these questions will determine many important features with respect to the bass and lead.

Above all, the answers to these questions will be your best guide as you endeavor to pick out the best notes to use in your lead. You will soon discover these by playing the lead instrument along with the drums and the bass. What happens with me is that certain important notes belonging to the chosen scale tend to present themselves, and from those a melodic idea tends to emerge, which I then develop and record. Once it is recorded, I can then edit it and crystallize it into a final form.

Leave Yourself Somewhere to Go

Once you have laid down the drum, bass, and lead material, you will have more or less the most important ingredients of the track. At this point it might be tempting to start sequencing and extending your track, although it would probably be unwise to do so. It would be far more useful to look ahead to see what else you will need for your track. What are you going to use in the way of contrasting material later in the track? Is the lead going to be presented with an accompaniment at some point?

The aim of layering is to set down as much material as possible without the additional complication of sequencing. The more layers you can lay down, the better. You can always mute the earlier layers you did and then work on some contrasting material, a subgroup of layers that will only be used later in the track.

The nature of these layers will be determined by the direction in which you can see the piece going in your imagination. As I mentioned in the previous chapter, musical structure is a juxtaposition of repetition and change. To be able to introduce change, you need a contrasting idea or another slant on the material you have already. This might involve a more ambient section using strings, pads, SFX, or samples. Whatever it involves, the time to develop this material is during the layering phase.

If you do not do this, you will start sequencing and find that you have left yourself nowhere to go in the piece. Your drums and bass have come in, and now you have introduced your lead. Where do you go from there? Taking out the drums for a while will not extend your track very far. Basically, you are stuck. So give yourself the option to go somewhere. This is like planning a journey in advance and anticipating what you will need on the journey. Look to SFX, too. What type of SFX would help to enhance the atmosphere of the music? Lay them down now so that you have them all ready and in hand.

During the layering stage, you can also be very intuitive and set up layers as and when they are sparked in your imagination. It doesn't even matter if it turns out that you do not use them. At least they are all there and ready for you should you require them. So be as imaginative and as inventive as you can at this stage and set up as many different layers as you can think of. Figure 18.7 shows an example of layering.

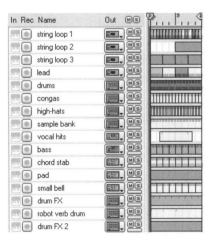

Figure 18.7   Initial layering of track.

Everything that is needed for the track is all there, just like a toolbox full of all of the right tools for the job. Through this process of layering, it has also been possible to make sure that everything works together and that there are no problems in terms of the overall sound. Any problems that do arise can easily be dealt with at this stage. A layer can be given less reverb, or you could use EQ to suppress the fat middle range of a pad sound. Once everything has been layered in this fashion, the track is now ready to be sequenced.

Sequencing Your Music

Through the process of layering, you have laid down everything that you could possibly imagine you might need for your track. Once you start sequencing, you might add more material later. But at the present time this is unimportant. What is important is that you have laid down sufficient material to create an entire track. You have your drums, bass, lead, pads and fills, accompaniment patterns, SFX, samples, riffs, and so on. Everything has been recorded, edited, quantized, and grooved, and appropriate insert FX have been applied where necessary. Everything is all there, waiting to be sequenced.

We are fortunate that the manufacturers of music software programs tend to offer us separate windows for the respective jobs of layering and sequencing. Layering is done in the editing windows—that is, the piano roll or staff view, where you can be aware of the recorded pitch content, the velocity curves, and the applied control data. Within this window you can edit each layer and prepare it for its final form. Sequencing, on the other hand, is done in the Arrange window, where your material is blocked or grouped into separate clips that can be copied, pasted, and shifted around as you develop the structure of the piece.

Sequencing is rather like opening up a telescope. You are now engaged in the job of opening up and extending the layers. In Figure 18.8, you can see the layers presented in Figure 18.7 in their final sequenced form.

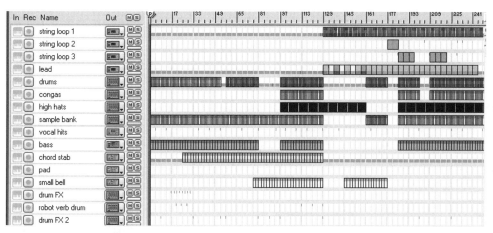

Figure 18.8 Sequenced layers.

So, your first job is to envision how the track is going to open up. To do this, you need to be aware of what the track is heading toward. Where is it going? What is it leading to? The answers to these questions will be determined by what you feel to be the best and most powerful parts of the music. These will represent your high points.

It is a great mistake to present the high points too early. If you do, the track will have nowhere to go from there except down. For the high points to have the maximum impact, you must build up to them. Generally, these occur about two-thirds of the way through the track. After you reach this point, it is then a matter of slowly winding down to the end of the track. So make your listener wait for the high points. Build up gradually and create a sense of anticipation of the intended peaks.

Opportunities for a build are always there. How about introducing just the ride element of your drums first and then later bringing in the snare and kick? And rather than introducing an element straight away, fade it in over a series of, say, eight bars. Use a filter to introduce your bass so that it gradually emerges into the musical texture. There are all sorts of ways to bring your material in and create a paced sense of anticipation. Remember, less is more. It is often not so much the material that you use, but the way in which you use it.

You can also discover a lot by soloing various groups of elements to see how they sound together. In this way, you can develop some good ideas for later sections of the track. Realize that at any given moment, you will never need more than about three main elements. The human ear is not really capable of focusing on any more. Of the three, one will tend to be heard as foreground, one as middle ground, and the third as background. Listeners do not generally appreciate lots of elements all jostling for the foreground position. So decide which element is going to be in the foreground and subdue the others.

Final Editing

Once you have arranged your material into a viable and working structure, you can then do the job of the final edit. This involves making whatever changes you feel are appropriate. You might want to introduce a variation on your original drum pattern or insert some random changes to your hi-hat pattern here and there so it does not sound so looped and repetitive. You might feel some sections just have too much repetition, so you need to cut those down to an appropriate size. In the case of Figure 18.9, the velocity lane of a track has been opened, ready for some editing of the otherwise too-uniform velocities of the individual sounds.

It is often a good idea to leave the piece for a while after you sequence it. Your ears are probably fatigued by hearing the same material too much, and this fatigue might impair

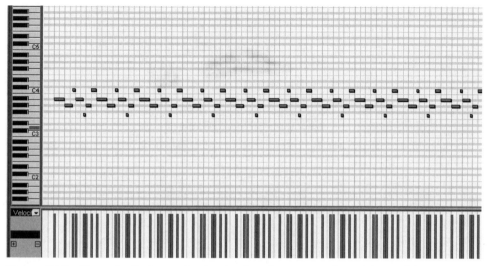

Figure 18.9 The velocity lane of a track, already open and awaiting editing.

your judgment. So go off and write something else and then come back to this track in a week or so. By then you will feel refreshed, and you will view the piece differently. Whereas before you saw only weaknesses and defects, you can now see great strength and originality. That fresh state of mind when you come back to the track is ideal for the purposes of final editing.

Conclusion

This chapter has talked about the usefulness of approaching the layering and sequencing of your music as separate processes. By layering your material first, you record everything you are going to need for your track and ensure that everything works together just fine. You can also edit individual layers at this stage. To do so once you have sequenced your music can be a waste of valuable time, since you might have to edit some four or five repetitions of the same material. Having layered your music, you can then experiment with various combinations of layered elements that you might use later in the track. Sequencing is the process that deals with extending those layers into a complete structure. Because the various blocks of material or clips to be used have already been laid down, this can often simply be a matter of copying and pasting the clips at the required point.

Having gotten to this stage, it is time to go on to the final stage of the creative process—mixing and mastering your track—which is the topic of the next chapter.

19 Mixing and Mastering

Mixing and mastering are quite separate jobs. The concern of mixing is getting the levels of individual tracks just right, securing an appropriate place for them within the stereo field, and applying EQ diagnostically to create an absolutely clear sound. The concern of mastering is creating a high-quality master recording suitable for use within particular environments, such as television, radio, commercially released CDs, and so on.

In a professional recording studio, the processes of mixing and mastering are done by separate professional people. The producer mixes the track, and the mastering engineer masters it. Computer musicians, however, are probably working from their home studios on an extremely tight budget. This means that they will probably have to do some of the jobs involved in this process entirely on their own (see Figure 19.1). Yet bear in mind that a skilled mix or mastering engineer probably spent years at university, coupled with many more years of gaining hard experience of the job. Can you match that? Probably not, in which case I would recommend leaving at least the mastering process to the professionals.

Mixing the Track: Levels

When mixing the levels of the track, you are adjusting the volume sliders of your mixer until you feel that they are in just the right positions. This job would not normally include fading in and out, as this process you would have already thought about and automated during the sequencing phase. The levels of the track need to be carefully adjusted relative to the track that has the highest level in the piece of music. This is nearly always the kick drum. Ideally, the kick drum should have the optimum output of 0 decibels. Anything over this level, as far as the use of software mixers is concerned, will cause clipping.

Some styles of music are incredibly hard to mix in this fashion. Drum and bass is noted for its sonic delivery and power. Because of this, those learning to write drum and bass tend to always try to squeeze out the maximum possible power from the sound that they can. They want that sub-bass to literally vibrate the walls of the club. So what happens

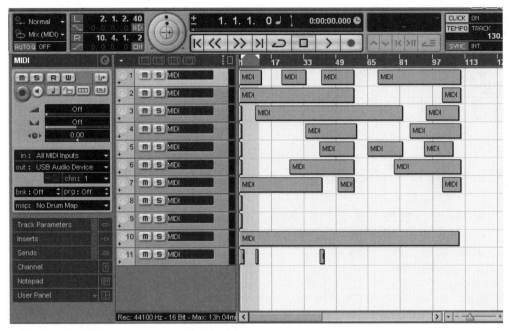

Figure 19.1   A Cubase project, already sequenced and awaiting mixing.

is that when mixing, the volume sliders start to creep up. This causes other parts to be too quiet, so their sliders come up, and so it goes on. In the end everything is mashing out at the highest possible level and producing what can only be described as a total mess. This only occurs because they are mixing their music with the sound of already mastered tracks in their minds and trying to match those levels during the pre-mastering phase. Suffice it to say, once you have got the kick at the optimum level, decide the level of everything else relative to it. And above all, try to resist the disease of slideritis. At the mixing stage, what you are trying to achieve is a total clarity of sound. Every track should be clearly heard and perfectly defined.

Another common mistake is to try to bring everything up into the foreground. What then happens is that the foreground becomes a battleground for supremacy between too many layers of music. This ruins all of the layers and prevents them from having a proper impact upon the track. So be clear as to what layer is intended to be the foreground, and mix down the other elements accordingly. To achieve this, don't be afraid of turning the slider right down on a layer if necessary.

In Figure 19.2, you can see the mixing platform offered by the Ableton program. Because of its use of color and well-defined visual elements, it offers a platform that is both easy to use and a pleasure to work with.

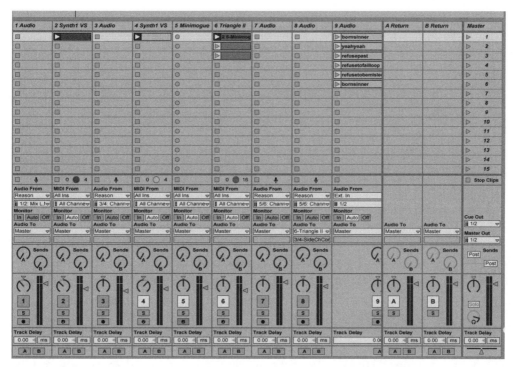

Figure 19.2 Ableton Live's mixing platform. The Ableton program offers a great platform for mixing your tracks. The panning controls have directional indicators that make it easy to discern the placement of each track in the stereo field. The volume sliders are clearly marked, and there is the added boon of being able to create track delay. This is really useful for creating wide, expansive sounds with the same sound being placed on two tracks, one panned left and the other right. One of the tracks is then given a slight delay.

Mixing the Track: Panning

Panning concerns the placement of the sound in the stereo field. It works in conjunction with effects, such as reverb and delay, to create that sense of width and space in which the music is heard. This sense is primarily generated along two main axes: to the front and back (reverb) and to the left and right (panpot). Figure 19.3 illustrates this.

While mixing your track, bear in mind that every sound you use in a composition will be given its own particular place in this field. The place each sound is given will often determine whether the final mix sounds clear or unclear. Here it is necessary to distinguish between the use of panning as a local effect and the use of panning in the mixing process. As an effect, panning processes are local to the tracks on which they are used.

A good example is an ethnic percussion pattern. When writing such a pattern, you would take panning into account in order to give maximum clarity and directional

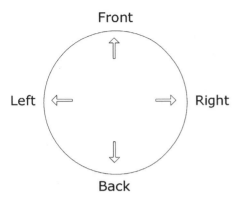

Figure 19.3   The two axes of the spatial field.

orientation to each individual drum sound. You would accomplish this by using a picture of the performers in your mind. Where are they relative to the center? You would then employ a panning strategy to reflect this mental image.

The same goes with your drum track. If you are facing the drums, imagine the directional sound each drum would come from. The snare would be slightly to the left, the hi-hats far left, the crash and ride on the right, while the toms would span right to left. You would normally do this kind of panning job when writing your drum track, rather than leaving it to the mixing stage. Having done this, your earlier decisions with regard to the panning would be taken into account when you pan the whole track. Panning the whole track is therefore a global as opposed to a local panning process.

Certain instruments tend to be always panned dead center. The drums and bass are a good example. However, I have known producers who have put the kick on two channels, one panned far left and the other panned far right. Although this tends to give the kick more impact, it does have the disadvantage of hogging the stereo field.

The next important consideration concerns instruments that play in similar frequency ranges. Without proper panning, these instruments will sound far less clear in the mix. It is surprising how often the solution to an unclear mix lies in the way in which it is panned. If there are two instruments operating within similar frequency ranges, one would be panned left and the other right. A good example is piano and guitar. In this way, they would complement and balance one another in the stereo field rather than competing with one another in a narrow range. This in turn would promote clarity in the mix. Both piano and guitar are clearly heard rather than competing with one another.

Balance is always a major concern when it comes to panning. You do not want too much on the left or too much on the right. You want a nice, balanced stereo field where each track has its own particular niche. Again, the keyword here is *clarity*. Although panning is a mixing tool, it also represents an integral feature of the composition—it is a compositional tool in its own right. Therefore, do not be afraid to experiment with panning effects. Using automation, it is possible to set up some quite intricate and amazing panning patterns, all of which can be used to add interest to your tracks—provided, of course, that you do not make your listener feel giddy or sick!

Mixing: EQ

Proper EQing is very much a matter for the professionals. It is certainly not something that can be grasped in a matter of weeks. A lot of study, research, and experimentation are required to be able to get the best out of EQ. And don't just research what the professionals have to say on the subject—back this up with experience. Take a sound —any sound—and try applying EQ to it. Hear what it sounds like when the lower frequencies are boosted or cut. Then go to the upper frequencies and listen carefully for the difference. And then try going up or down in the frequency spectrum. It will become apparent that a musical note is not like the symbol for it suggests—a neat little circle. On the contrary, it is a complex band of frequencies.

Experimenting with EQ will give you firsthand experience at finding out how these frequencies contribute to the sound—what the frequencies are that give the sound its strength, brightness, or noise content. You can do this kind of experimentation with a wide variety of musical sounds, drums, samples, and noises. Gradually, you will learn about the inner content of individual sounds and how particular frequencies contribute to their tonal quality. Once you have done this, you will be in a more knowledgeable position to apply EQ constructively to your work.

EQ is something many computer musicians worry unnecessarily about. This is probably because they have seen professional producers in recording studios applying EQ liberally to tracks. Yet the computer musician does not have the same type of problems as a professional producer. If a mic has been badly placed and it is impossible to do another take, the producer might try to manage the problem using EQ. But as pointed out earlier, the computer musician does not suffer this disadvantage. There is also a common misconception that EQ is like some kind of philosopher's stone that can turn every sound into gold. This is just not true. If you are working with bad sounds, EQ cannot turn them into good ones. The answer to this problem is to work with good sounds from the beginning and then just leave them alone.

Before we consider the process of EQing, look at Figure 19.4, which defines some of the basic terms that will be used. The diagrams serve as the best illustration of these terms.

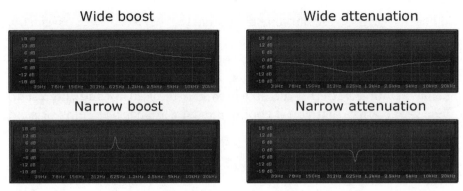

Figure 19.4 Basic EQing terms: wide, narrow, boost, attenuate.

Generally, EQ will be used in two ways. It will be used as a track doctor to diagnose and fix problems, and as a track enhancer, where it can be used to gently boost certain frequencies. In terms of the former, EQ devices can be used as diagnostic tools to discover the precise range of troublesome frequencies. Listen to the pad sound on audio Track 65 on the CD. A chord sounds continuously for 32 bars, and as it does so, a narrow band is boosted going up through the frequency spectrum. Note the way in which you can hear the individual frequencies being boosted. In the higher ranges, these sound like the whistling of a kettle. You can use this technique to locate troublesome frequencies and then you can cut them using a narrow band attenuation.

Some pads, for example, are just far too fat in the middle register, and they tend to clog the mix with midrange frequencies that are just not needed. An answer to this problem is to discover what the troublesome frequencies are and to attenuate them. The same goes with piano sounds, especially if the sustain pedal has been used. Yet the answer here might not necessarily be to EQ the sound, but to entirely remove the sustain pedal effect, go back into the edit window, and manually lengthen the piano notes so that they have sufficient length without use of the sustain pedal.

When mixing your track, you would first diagnose and fix such problems. This will leave you with a nice, clear mix with no mud, haze, noise, hiss, or whatever. Having done this, you would then consider what in the track might benefit from being boosted. And by boosted, I do not mean using EQ as a volume enhancer, because that is the job of your volume slider. I mean a very discrete and gentle boost applied to certain frequency ranges. Ideally, each instrument you use needs to sit comfortably within its own optimum frequency range. Provided that these ranges are not conflicting in any way, it is then possible to apply slight degrees of gentle and fairly wide boosting where you feel it is both safe and appropriate.

Mastering the Track

Once your track has been successfully mixed, it is then time to get it mastered. Mastering is the process in which the track is optimized for recording onto a particular medium, such as CD, vinyl, or tape. During the process of mastering, the track is polished and shaped in such a way that it not only has comparable levels to commercially produced recordings, but that it also shines at its very best.

The subject of mastering is a huge one, and it certainly goes beyond both the scope and the brevity of this particular book. Indeed, you would need a separate book in itself to cover the subject. The process of mastering is strictly a matter for the professionals. I have heard so many tracks totally ruined by the music producer who fancies having a tinker at mastering himself. If you do want to try this, then read up on it and by all means have a go. But make sure that you retain a copy of your original track during its pre-mastered phase. This way, if you do ruin it, you will always have the original to fall back on.

To master a track effectively requires not only a large amount of professional and expert knowledge, but also a huge rack of as many as 20 or 30 very expensive processors totally dedicated to the purposes of mastering. And it will take place in a specially tuned and adapted environment using the very best monitors that money can buy. Therefore, if you do write a good track and you think it might land you with a recording contract, get it professionally mastered. For this reason, it is imperative that once you have mixed the track, you should leave it alone. If you do try to master it, you could render it unusable for the purposes of professional mastering.

If you are interested in mastering your own material, most DAWs do offer limited facilities for mastering. But to do so would entail much study on the subject in order for you to be able to do a good job of it. A book that I would recommend is Bobby Owsinski's *The Mastering Engineer's Handbook, Second Edition: The Audio Mastering Handbook* (Course Technology PTR, 2007).

Conclusion

This chapter discussed the essential differences between the processes of mixing and mastering. It pointed out the necessity of acquiring a great deal of knowledge to be able to attain even a small degree of competence with regard to the processes of mixing and mastering. Acquiring this knowledge represents a rather steep learning curve and really is a separate branch of study in its own right. Until you have acquired such knowledge, I recommend that you consult the services of professionals, particularly during the mastering phase of the process.

Conclusion

Where to Next?

This book has taken you through much of the basic knowledge required to compose and produce music on your computer. Of course, over time you will develop your own approaches to everything we discussed. But when you're starting out on the endeavour to compose and produce your own music, it is at least helpful to receive the knowledge and advice of another. And even if you are an experienced songwriter, composer, or producer, there is always more to learn about your area.

If you are having some degree of success writing your own music, then of course the next issue is what to do with it. You might ultimately wish to produce music professionally, in which case the first thing is to get your music out there so it can be heard. Uploading your music to either MySpace or Facebook is a good way to start. This will offer your music the kind of exposure it requires, as well as give you the opportunity to obtain constructive feedback from an often sympathetic audience.

And by all means, send your music off to the A&R departments of suitable record companies. Despite the myths that surround this, they do and will listen to your tracks. This is because their future income depends upon the fact that somewhere, amongst that huge pile of demo CDs on their desks, lays the next big sound. It is consequently not in their best interest to trash material without first listening to it. Having listened to it, if the record company feels that they can make money from your tracks, you can be sure they will contact you. There is also the option of uploading your music to one of the many online record labels, such as GarageBand or BeatsDigital. You will receive a commission depending upon the number of times your track has been downloaded.

Another option is producing music for film, television, or computer games. The music produced for computer games accounts for more listening hours of music than any other media. So along with music for films and TV, it represents an important source of revenue for music composers. To obtain such work, you often need personal contact with the producer, although that is by no means vital. Another way into this is to send a varied portfolio of material to suitable producers. Should they like what they hear, they might contact you with regard to providing music for their next production.

Before you start to send any music out there, though, I recommend that you spend some time studying and researching the music business, in particular the codes and practices surrounding the copyrighting of material. This research is essential if you are not to be exploited or taken advantage of. Indeed, without it you will be like a lump of meat thrown into a pool full of sharks! So study the music business, find out its ways, and learn how to protect yourself from exploitation. Advantageously, there is a huge amount of information about this subject posted on the Internet. In particular learn how to copyright your music properly—that is, to use the appropriate signs, symbols, and copyright notices on your recordings. Although the copyright of your work automatically belongs to you as the originator, the posting of copyright notices both acts as a deterrent and demonstrates your awareness of copyright law.

It is also a good idea to join a collecting society, such as the Performing Rights Society of Great Britain. Membership in the PRS or its equivalent in your own country brings with it great benefits. For a one-time fee paid when you join, you can register and copyright your material with them, and they will also collect for you any royalties due as a result of public performances of your music. Whether your music gets played in a bar, a club, on the radio, or on TV, the collecting society will diligently collect those royalties and pay them into a designated bank account.

Regardless of whether you try to sell your music, try not to base your entire output on the successful imitation of styles that are already out there. If you do, although your friends and family might encourage you and say that your music sounds just like music they have heard on the radio, realistically speaking this means that the niche for that particular market has probably already been filled. So why would record companies want even more of it? What they are often looking for is a new, fresh sound that can be developed, promoted, and marketed. If you imitate what is already out there, you are just producing more of the same. So rather than only looking outward for cues to develop your own music, try also looking inward at your own unique and personal vision of the way music should sound. And wherever possible, try to remain true to that vision, to be original—that is writing music with your own unique voice.

Index